SPECTRUM
Test Practice
Grade 4

Published by Spectrum
an imprint of
Frank Schaffer Publications®

SPECTRUM

Editors: Sara Bierling and Kathryn Wheeler

Frank Schaffer Publications®

Spectrum is an imprint of Frank Schaffer Publications.

Send all inquiries to:
Frank Schaffer Publications
3195 Wilson Drive NW
Grand Rapids, Michigan 49534

Spectrum Test Practice—grade 4

ISBN: 1-57768-974-7

5 6 7 8 9 10 11 12 POH 11 10 09 08 07 06

With increased accountability in ensuring academic success for all learners, testing now takes a significant amount of time for students in all settings. Standardized tests are designed to measure what students know. These tests are nationally normed. State tests are usually tied to specific academic standards identified for mastery.

For many students, testing can be a mystery. They fear not doing well and not knowing what to expect on the test. This *Spectrum Test Practice* book was developed to introduce students to both the format and the content they will encounter on tests. It was developed on the assumption that students have received prior instruction on the skills included. This book is designed to cover the content on a representative sample of state standards. The sampling of standards is found on pages 8–10 with a correlation to the skills covered in this book and a correlation to sample standardized tests. Spaces are provided to record the correlation to the tests being administered by the user of this book. Spaces are also provided to add standards that are specific to the user.

Features of *Spectrum Test Practice*

- Skill lessons, sample tests for subtopics, and comprehensive content area tests
- Clues for being successful with specific skills
- Correlation of skills to state standards and standardized tests
- Format and structure similar to other formal tests
- Written response required in the Science and Social Studies sections
- Reproducible for use by a teacher for a classroom

Overview

This book is developed within content areas (Reading, Language, Math, Science, and Social Studies). A comprehensive practice test follows at the end of the content area, with an answer sheet for students to record responses. Within each content area, specific subtopics have been identified. Sample tests are provided for each subtopic. Within each subtopic, specific skill lessons are presented. These specific skill lessons include an example and a clue for being successful with the skill.

Comprehensive Practice Test

A comprehensive practice test is provided for each content area. The subtopics for each area are identified below:

- **Reading**
    - Vocabulary (synonyms, antonyms, word meanings, multi-meaning words, root words, affixes, and words in context)
    - Reading Comprehension (main idea, recalling details, sequencing, inferencing, drawing conclusions, fact and opinion, cause and effect, and author's purpose in fiction and nonfiction articles)

- **Language**
    - Language Mechanics (capitalization and punctuation)
    - Language Expression (usage, sentences, and paragraphs)
    - Spelling (both correct and incorrect spelling)
    - Study Skills (dictionary skills, reference materials, reading tables and graphs, book parts)

- **Math**
  - Concepts (numeration, number concepts, fractions and decimals, algebra, properties)
  - Computation (addition and subtraction of whole numbers, fractions, and decimals; multiplication and division of whole numbers)
  - Applications (geometry, measurement, and problem solving)
- **Science***
  - Electricity/Magnetism
  - Plant and Animal Structures
  - Water/Weather Cycles
  - Human Body
  - Astronomy
- **Social Studies***
  - United States Regions
  - State History
  - World Regions/Climates
  - Map Skills
  - Economics

*Since states and often districts determine units of study within Science and Social Studies, the content in this book may not be aligned with the content offered in all courses of study. The content within each area is grade level appropriate. It is based on a sampling of state standards. The tests in Science and Social Studies include both multiple choice and written answer.

Comprehensive Practice Test Includes

- Content Area (i.e. Language)
- Subtopics (i.e. Language Mechanics)
- Directions, examples, and test questions
- Separate answer sheet with "bubbles" to be filled in for answers

Sample Tests

Sample tests are included for all subtopics. These sample tests are designed to apply the knowledge and experience from the skill lessons in a more formal format. No clues are included. These sample tests are shorter than the comprehensive tests and longer than the skill lessons. The skills on the test items are presented in the same order as introduced in the book.

Sample Tests Include

- Subtopic (i.e. Language Mechanics)
- Directions, examples, and test questions

Skill Lessons

Skill lessons include sample questions and clues for mastering the skill. The questions are formatted as they generally appear in tests, whether the tests are standardized and nationally normed or state specific.

Skill Lessons Include

- Subtopic (i.e. Language Mechanics)
- Skill (i.e. Punctuation)
- Directions and examples
- Clues for completing the activity
- Practice questions

Use

This book can be used in a variety of ways, depending on the needs of the students. Some examples follow:

- Review the skills correlation on pages 8–10. Record the skills tested in your state and/or district on the blanks provided.
- Administer the comprehensive practice test for each content area. Have students use the sample answer sheet in order to simulate the actual testing experience. The tests for Reading, Language, and Math are multiple choice. Evaluate the results.

- Administer the sample test for the subtopics within the content area. Evaluate the results.

- Administer the specific skill lessons for those students needing additional practice with content. Evaluate the results.

- Use the skill lessons as independent work in centers, for homework, or as seatwork.

- Prepare an overhead transparency of skill lessons to be presented to a group of students. Use the transparency to model the skill and provide guided practice.

- Send home the Letter to Parent/Guardian found on page 7.

Clues for Getting Started

Determine the structure for implementing *Spectrum Test Practice*. These questions may help guide you:

- Do you want to assess the overall performance of your class in each academic area? If so, reproduce the practice test and sample answer sheet for each area. Use the results to determine subtopics that need additional instruction and/or practice.

- Do you already have information about the overall achievement of your students within each academic area? Do you need more information about their achievement within subtopics, such as Vocabulary within Reading? If so, reproduce the sample tests for the subtopics.

- Do your students need additional practice with some of the specific skills that they will encounter on the standardized test? Do you need to know which students have mastered which skills? These skill lessons provide opportunities for instruction and practice.

- Go over the purpose of tests with your students. Describe the tests and the testing situation, explaining that the tests are often timed, that answers are recorded on a separate answer sheet, and that the questions cover material they have studied.

- Do some of the skill lessons together to help students develop strategies for selecting answers and for different types of questions. Use the "clues" for learning strategies for test taking.

- Make certain that students know how to mark a separate answer sheet. Use the practice test and answer sheet so that they are familiar with the process.

- Review the directions for each test. Identify key words that students must use to answer the questions. Do the sample test questions with the class.

- Remind students to answer each question, to budget their time so they can complete all the questions, and to apply strategies for determining answers.

Reduce the mystery of taking tests for your students. By using *Spectrum Test Practice*, you have the materials that show them what the tests will look like, what kinds of questions are on the tests, and ways to help them be more successful taking tests.

Note: The comprehension questions in reading in all selections are in the same order: main idea, recalling details/sequencing, inferencing/drawing conclusions, fact and opinion/cause and effect. This information can be used to diagnose areas for needed instruction.

Note: If you wish to time your students on a practice test, we suggest allowing 1.25 minutes per question for this grade level.

Dear Parent/Guardian:

We will be giving tests to measure your child's learning. These tests include questions that relate to the information your child is learning in school. The tests may be standardized and used throughout the nation, or they may be specific to our state. Regardless of the test, the results are used to measure student achievement.

Many students do not test well even though they know the material. They may not test well because of test anxiety or the mystery of taking tests. What will the test look like? What will some of the questions be? What happens if I do not do well?

To help your child do his/her best on the tests, we will be using some practice tests. These tests help your child learn what the tests will look like, what some of the questions might be, and ways to learn to take tests. These practice tests will be included as part of your child's homework.

You can help your child with this important part of learning. Below are some suggestions:

- Ask your child if he/she has homework.
- Provide a quiet place to work.
- Go over the work with your child.
- Use a timer to help your child learn to manage his/her time when taking tests.
- Tell your child he/she is doing a good job.
- Remind him/her to use the clues that are included in the lessons.

If your child is having difficulty with the tests, these ideas may be helpful:

- Review the examples.
- Skip the difficult questions and come back to them later.
- Guess at those that you do not know.
- Answer all the questions.

By showing you are interested in how your child is doing, he/she will do even better in school. Enjoy this time with your child. Good luck with the practice tests.

Sincerely,

● **Grade 4**

Sample Standards	Spectrum Test Practice Gr. 4	*CAT Level for Gr. 4	**CTBS Level for Gr. 4	Other	Other	Other
Reading						
Vocabulary						
Using Synonyms	X	X	X			
Using Antonyms	X		X			
Using Homographs	X					
Using Idioms						
Using Multi-Meaning Words	X	X				
Using Context Clues	X	X				
Using Common Roots and Word Parts	X					
Other						
Comprehension						
Identifying Main Idea	X	X	X			
Identifying Supporting Details	X	X	X			
Identifying Sequence of Events	X	X	X			
Drawing Conclusions	X	X	X			
Making Predictions	X	X	X			
Comparing and Contrasting	X	X	X			
Identifying Cause and Effect	X	X				
Identifying Character Traits/Feelings	X	X	X			
Identifying Story Parts	X					
Distinguishing Between Fact and Opinion	X					
Using Graphic Organizers		X	X			
Understanding Figurative Language		X	X			
Summarizing	X	X	X			
Identifying Author's Purpose	X	X				
Reading Various Genres	X	X				
Other						
Language						
Mechanics						
Expression						
Using Correct Capitalization and Punctuation	X	X	X			
Determining Correct Usage	X	X	X			
Recognizing Simple Subjects and Predicates	X		X			
Combining Sentences	X	X	X			
Using Simple and Compound Sentences		X	X			
Identifying Topic Sentences for Paragraphs	X	X	X			
Identifying Supporting Sentences for Paragraphs	X	X	X			
Other						
Spelling						
Identifying Correct Spelling	X		X			
Identifying Incorrect Spelling	X		X			
Other						

* Terra Nova CAT™ ©2001 CTB/McGraw-Hill
** Terra Nova CTBS® ©1997 CTB/McGraw-Hill

● Grade 4

Sample Standards	Spectrum Test Practice Gr. 4	*CAT Level for Gr. 4	**CTBS Level for Gr. 4	Other	Other	Other
Study Skills						
Using Reference Materials	X	X				
Interpreting Graphs and Tables	X					
Using Books Parts	X					
Using Graphic Organizers	X					
Reading Maps	X					
Other						
Math						
Concepts						
Numeration						
Using Number Lines	X	X				
Using Numbers Up To 1,000,000	X	X				
Rounding Whole Numbers Up To 10,000						
Ordering and Comparing Whole Numbers	X		X			
Renaming Whole Numbers As Fractions						
Using Mixed Numbers and Improper Fractions	X					
Using Place Value	X	X				
Other						
Algebra						
Recognizing Patterns with Pictures		X	X			
Extending Number Patterns	X	X	X			
Using Number Sentences	X	X	X			
Using Symbols To Represent Numbers	X	X	X			
Other						
Fractions and Decimals						
Writing 10ths and 100ths In Fraction and Decimal Notation	X					
Rounding Decimals	X					
Ordering Fractions and Decimals	X					
Adding and Subtracting Fractions and Decimals Using Pictures or Objects		X				
Recognizing Fractions and Decimals from Pictures	X	X				
Other						
Computation						
Whole Numbers						
Using Standard Algorithms for Operations	X	X	X			
Using Mental Arithmetic for Adding and Subtracting Rounded Numbers	X					
Estimating	X	X	X			
Other						
Fractions and Decimals						
Adding and Subtracting Fractions and Decimals Using Pictures or Objects		X	X			
Using Standard Algorithms for Adding and Subtracting Decimals	X	X	X			
Other						

* Terra Nova CAT™ ©2001 CTB/McGraw-Hill
** Terra Nova CTBS® ©1997 CTB/McGraw-Hill

● Grade 4

Sample Standards	Spectrum Test Practice Gr. 4	*CAT Level for Gr. 4	**CTBS Level for Gr. 4	Other	Other	Other
Probability						
Interpreting Data	X		X			
Other						
Applications						
Geometry						
Identifying Lines, Angles, and Shapes	X	X	X			
Identifying Lines of Symmetry	X	X				
Identifying Congruent Figures	X					
Other						
Measurement						
Estimating						
Measuring to Nearest Eighth-inch and Millimeter		X	X			
Renaming Feet to Inches and Meters to Centimeters	X					
Finding Perimeter and Area of Squares and Rectangles	X	X	X			
Using Volume, Mass, and Capacity	X	X				
Adding Time Intervals	X					
Making Change	X					
Other						
Problem Solving						
Selecting Appropriate Operations	X	X	X			
Using a Variety of Methods to Solve Problems, Including Graphs, Tables, and Charts	X	X	X			
Identifying Relevant and Irrelevant Information	X		X			
Estimating Results	X		X			
Selecting Reasonable Solutions	X					
Calculating Multi-step Problems	X	X	X			
Other						
Science						
Understanding the Concept of Recycling		X	X			
Comparing Fresh and Ocean Waters		X				
Understanding Light and Heat	X	X	X			
Understanding Magnetism	X	X				
Understanding Plant and Animal Structures	X	X	X			
Understanding Earth/Sun Relationships	X	X	X			
Understanding the Water Cycle			X			
Other						
Social Studies						
Understanding the History of the State	X					
Identifying the Branches of Government		X	X			
Understanding the Geography of the State Region	X					
Applying the Basic Vocabulary of Economics	X		X			
Interpreting Maps/Graphic Organizers	X	X	X			
Interpreting Time Lines		X	X			
Other						

* Terra Nova CAT™   ©2001 CTB/McGraw-Hill
** Terra Nova CTBS®   ©1997 CTB/McGraw-Hill

Published by Spectrum. Copyright protected.

1-57768-974-7 *Spectrum Test Practice 4*

READING: VOCABULARY

● Lesson 1: Synonyms

Directions: Read each item. Choose the word that means the same or about the same as the underlined word.

Examples

A. fast <u>vehicle</u>
- (A) runner
- (B) animal
- (C) car
- (D) computer

B. To be <u>healthy</u> is to be —
- (F) slow
- (G) well
- (H) active
- (J) ill

 Clue Make sure you look at the <u>underlined</u> word.
Fill in the circle next to the <u>synonym</u>.

● Practice

1. attend a <u>conference</u>
- (A) party
- (B) game
- (C) meeting
- (D) race

2. <u>beautiful</u> painting
- (F) pretty
- (G) interesting
- (H) colorful
- (J) light

3. <u>repair</u> the car
- (A) clean
- (B) drive
- (C) fix
- (D) sell

4. <u>thin</u> slice
- (F) short
- (G) skinny
- (H) long
- (J) wide

5. To <u>rush</u> through your homework is to —
- (A) relax
- (B) slow
- (C) finish
- (D) hurry

6. <u>Raw</u> vegetables are —
- (F) uncooked
- (G) green
- (H) smelly
- (J) young

7. A <u>dim</u> light bulb is —
- (A) dull
- (B) bright
- (C) unintelligent
- (D) new

8. To walk <u>quickly</u> is to walk —
- (F) confidently
- (G) carefully
- (H) rapidly
- (J) happily

STOP

READING: VOCABULARY

● Lesson 2: Vocabulary Skills

Directions: Read each item. Choose the word that means the same or about the same as the underlined word.

Examples

A. detect a clue

- (A) to find
- (B) to hide
- (C) to enjoy
- (D) to make up

B. She had to select the book for the next meeting. To select is to —

- (F) find
- (G) review
- (H) read
- (J) choose

Clue Make sure you look at the underlined word. Eliminate answer choices you know are wrong.

● Practice

1. venomous snake

- (A) vicious
- (B) poisonous
- (C) sharp
- (D) huge

2. encourage friends

- (F) fascinate
- (G) worry
- (H) cheer up
- (J) disappoint

3. mature person

- (A) grown-up
- (B) dying
- (C) new
- (D) green

4. The teacher was irritated. Irritated means —

- (F) excited
- (G) helpful
- (H) annoyed
- (J) boring

5. His pants were baggy. Baggy means —

- (A) loose
- (B) brown
- (C) too small
- (D) made of cotton

6. He was the first conductor of the train. A conductor is a —

- (F) driver
- (G) janitor
- (H) owner
- (J) rider

7. Sharon was elated when she won. Elated means —

- (A) grim
- (B) joyful
- (C) outside
- (D) unpleasant

STOP

READING: VOCABULARY

● **Lesson 3: Antonyms**

Directions: Read each item. Choose the word that means the opposite of the underlined word.

Examples

A. The tortoise took a <u>leisurely</u> walk.
- (A) lovely
- (B) swift
- (C) leathery
- (D) delicious

B. <u>recall</u> information
- (F) forget
- (G) remember
- (H) write
- (J) find

 If you are not sure which answer is correct, take your best guess. Eliminate answer choices you know are incorrect.

● **Practice**

1. Leslie was <u>disappointed</u> when it rained.
   - (A) saddened
   - (B) pleased
   - (C) relieved
   - (D) entertained

2. The car was <u>fast</u>.
   - (F) shallow
   - (G) sluggish
   - (H) speedy
   - (J) rabbit

3. The dog's fur felt <u>silky</u>.
   - (A) soft
   - (B) smooth
   - (C) rough
   - (D) dirty

4. Banana slugs are <u>moist</u> to the touch.
   - (F) dry
   - (G) slimy
   - (H) rough
   - (J) rubbery

5. <u>rough</u> board
   - (A) large
   - (B) heavy
   - (C) smooth
   - (D) long

6. <u>docile</u> animal
   - (F) vicious
   - (G) gentle
   - (H) shy
   - (J) active

7. <u>active</u> child
   - (A) immobile
   - (B) exhausted
   - (C) bored
   - (D) thrilled

8. left <u>promptly</u>
   - (F) late
   - (G) recently
   - (H) quietly
   - (J) slowly

STOP

READING: VOCABULARY

● Lesson 4: Multi-Meaning Words

Example

For items A and 1–2, choose the answer in which the underlined word is used in the same way as the sentence in the box.

For items 3–5, read the two sentences with blanks. Choose the word that fits best in both sentences.

A. | Please file these papers. |

- (A) The counselor pulled out her file on the Jones family.
- (B) Sally used a file to smooth her fingernails.
- (C) I put the file cards in order.
- (D) Jane asked her secretary to file the reports on water safety.

 Clue If a question is too difficult, skip it and come back to it later if you have time.

● Practice

1. | I used a lemon to make lemonade. |

- (A) The color of the baby's room is lemon.
- (B) That car was a lemon.
- (C) This cleaner has a lovely lemon scent.
- (D) Rachel bought a lemon at the store.

2. | She could never reach the right note on the piano. |

- (F) Please make a note of this change.
- (G) I wrote a note so you will not forget.
- (H) The musical note he asked us to play was C.
- (J) Note the large size of the buildings.

3. Do you feel _____ ?
   We get our water from a _____ .
- (A) well
- (B) good
- (C) pipe
- (D) sick

4. Mrs. Johnson said Carrie was a _____ student.
   The light from the headlights was _____ .
- (F) noisy
- (G) red
- (H) bright
- (J) hard working

5. The surface of the car was _____ .
   Mr. Abed gave a _____ speech.
- (A) dirty
- (B) shiny
- (C) painted
- (D) dull

STOP

READING: VOCABULARY

● **Lesson 5: Words in Context**

Directions: Read the paragraph. Choose the word that fits best in each numbered blank.

Examples

In-line skating might be the fastest-growing _____(A) in America. Typical _____(B) follow roads, sidewalks, or bike paths. This sport is relatively new, but it is already enjoyed by people young and old.

A.
- (A) thing
- (B) people
- (C) town
- (D) sport

B.
- (F) skaters
- (G) vehicles
- (H) hikers
- (J) results

● **Practice** **Clue** Read the passage once. Then read each sentence with a blank carefully. Use the meaning of the sentence to find the answer.

Glass is an amazing substance. Made by heating sand with a few other simple chemicals, glass is both _____(1) and beautiful. In the _____(2), you drink your juice in a glass. At your school, you may _____(3) the building through a glass door. The lights inside the school are made of glass, as is the _____(4) of the computer you will use. If you go to gym class, the basketball backboard might even be made of glass. Your family may have pieces of glass as decorations around the house, and if you go to a _____(5), you might see _____(6) glass from hundreds of years ago.

1.
- (A) ugly
- (B) useful
- (C) cloudy
- (D) thin

2.
- (F) evening
- (G) time
- (H) morning
- (J) mood

3.
- (A) open
- (B) see
- (C) like
- (D) enter

4.
- (F) inside
- (G) keyboard
- (H) screen
- (J) mouse

5.
- (A) aquarium
- (B) bus stop
- (C) gas station
- (D) museum

6.
- (F) new
- (G) antique
- (H) full
- (J) broken

STOP

READING: VOCABULARY

● Lesson 6: Word Study

Directions: Read each item. Choose the answer you think is correct.

Examples

A. Which of these words probably comes from the Latin word *circuitus*, meaning *a going around*?

- (A) circus
- (B) circuit
- (C) cirrus
- (D) circa

B. Let's _____ the ripe apples. Which word means to *gather* the ripe apples?

- (F) eat
- (G) collect
- (H) check
- (J) sell

 Clue Mark the correct answer as soon as you find it.

● Practice

1. Which of these words probably comes from the Greek word *logos*, meaning *word or speech*?

- (A) locate
- (B) logo
- (C) lodge
- (D) log

2. Which of these words probably comes from the French word *ravager*, meaning to *uproot*?

- (F) ravage
- (G) ravel
- (H) rave
- (J) ravine

3. The owner had to _____ the puppy for chewing the shoes. Which word means to *speak harshly*?

- (A) scold
- (B) pursue
- (C) alert
- (D) inspire

4. José _____ his report to include a section on bugs. Which word means he *changed it* by adding something?

- (F) wrote
- (G) amended
- (H) erased
- (J) corrected

For items 5–6, choose the answer that best defines the underlined part.

5. wonder<u>ful</u>   mouth<u>ful</u>

- (A) to be doing
- (B) full of
- (C) outside
- (D) underneath

6. <u>mis</u>take   <u>mis</u>lead

- (F) correctly
- (G) before
- (H) to do after
- (J) wrongly

 STOP

Name _____ Date _____

Examples

For items A and 1–4, choose the word that means the same or about the same as the underlined word.

A.   calm <u>ocean</u>

   (A) water

   (B) sea

   (C) lake

   (D) body

For items B and 5–8, read each item. Choose the answer you think is correct.

B.   <u>Infect</u> means—

   (F) to act

   (G) to cheer up

   (H) to spread disease

   (J) to discover

---

1. <u>high</u> fence

   (A) tall

   (B) happy

   (C) long

   (D) wide

2. <u>paste</u> the paper

   (F) fold

   (G) attach

   (H) patch

   (J) glue

3. <u>fix</u> the car

   (A) polish

   (B) repair

   (C) sell

   (D) buy

4. <u>chilly</u> day

   (F) long

   (G) frozen

   (H) cold

   (J) unpleasant

5. If something is moving <u>swiftly</u>, it is moving —

   (A) slowly

   (B) smoothly

   (C) quickly

   (D) on the land

6. <u>Shallow</u> means —

   (F) not intelligent

   (G) deep

   (H) not deep

   (J) able to swim

7. To <u>remain</u> is to —

   (A) stay

   (B) leave early

   (C) go to the middle

   (D) do over again

8. That store was the <u>nearest</u>.

   (F) the most distant

   (G) biggest

   (H) best

   (J) the closest

GO ON

Name _____ Date _____

For items 9–13, choose the meaning for each underlined word.

9. The wings of the butterflies were <u>fluttering</u> in the breeze.
   Fluttering means —
   - (A) waving
   - (B) colorful
   - (C) lovely
   - (D) flashing

10. Gazelles and impalas are <u>prey</u> to the cheetah.
    Prey means —
    - (F) food
    - (G) friends
    - (H) similar
    - (J) predators

11. David gave his sister a <u>smirk</u>.
    Smirk means —
    - (A) friendly smile
    - (B) scar
    - (C) smug expression
    - (D) facemask

12. We were <u>exhausted</u> after running.
    Exhausted means —
    - (F) very tired
    - (G) refreshed
    - (H) excited
    - (J) wide awake

13. I <u>sprinted</u> to the finish line.
    Sprinted means —
    - (A) skipped
    - (B) crawled
    - (C) ran very quickly
    - (D) tripped

For items 14–19, choose the word that means the opposite of the underlined word.

14. <u>valuable</u> painting
    - (F) strange
    - (G) expensive
    - (H) worthless
    - (J) humorous

15. <u>loose</u> tie
    - (A) tight
    - (B) lost
    - (C) plain
    - (D) ill fitting

16. <u>narrow</u> ledge
    - (F) thin
    - (G) cement
    - (H) skinny
    - (J) wide

17. We <u>always</u> use this road to go to school.
    - (A) never
    - (B) sometimes
    - (C) usually
    - (D) frequently

18. The workers wanted to <u>unpack</u> the truck.
    - (F) carry
    - (G) pack
    - (H) remove
    - (J) move

19. Tom was <u>awake</u> most of the night.
    - (A) up
    - (B) asleep
    - (C) restless
    - (D) watching TV

GO ON

Name _____ Date _____

For items 20–23, read the two sentences with blanks. Choose the word that fits best in both sentences.

20. The sun _____ at 5:45.
A _____ grew beside the steps.

- (F) appeared
- (G) rose
- (H) flower
- (J) set

21. It's not safe to _____ a boat.
This _____ is too heavy to move.

- (A) sink
- (B) stone
- (C) push
- (D) rock

22. What _____ will you be on vacation?
I enjoy eating _____ .

- (F) days
- (G) fruit
- (H) weeks
- (J) dates

23. The captain took _____ of the ship.
The cavalry made a great _____ .

- (A) yell
- (B) charge
- (C) control
- (D) run

24. Follow the deer tracks.

In which sentence does the word tracks mean the same thing as in the sentence above?

- (F) The train moved swiftly on the tracks.
- (G) Gerald tracks satellites for the government.
- (H) The dog made tracks in the snow.
- (J) Never stop your car on the train tracks.

25. Hand me that green plant.

In which sentence does the word plant mean the same thing as in the sentence above?

- (A) The electric plant was a busy place to work.
- (B) Plant those bushes here.
- (C) They used Joe as a plant to spy on the kids.
- (D) I gave Mom a plant for Mother's Day.

For items 26–27, choose the answer that best defines the underlined part.

26. motherless   painless

- (F) with
- (G) like
- (H) more
- (J) without

27. magnify   magnificent

- (A) magnetic
- (B) great
- (C) smaller
- (D) open

GO ON

READING: VOCABULARY
SAMPLE TEST (cont.)

28. Which of these words probably comes from the Latin word *lampein*, meaning to *shine*?

- (F) lampoon
- (G) lament
- (H) lamp
- (J) lamprey

29. Which of these words probably comes from the Middle English word *wose*, meaning *juice*?

- (A) ooze
- (B) worst
- (C) wowser
- (D) wound

30. _____, Mom had forgotten the can opener.
Which of these words means that it was *unlucky*?

- (F) Fortunately
- (G) Mournfully
- (H) Excitedly
- (J) Unfortunately

31. Dave _____ around the room.
Which of these words means that he *walked in a bragging manner*?

- (A) tiptoed
- (B) strutted
- (C) ran
- (D) skipped

Read the paragraph. Choose the word that fits best in each numbered blank.

Leslie is becoming _____(32). People know about her art and her athletics. She is _____(33) in the music department for her skills. I'm really _____(34) of what she's done.

32.
- (F) famous
- (G) released
- (H) exhausted
- (J) fragile

33.
- (A) disliked
- (B) prepared
- (C) respected
- (D) always

34.
- (F) confused
- (G) rejected
- (H) lessened
- (J) proud

STOP

READING: READING COMPREHENSION

● Lesson 7: Main Idea

Directions: Read the passage. Choose the best answer to the questions that follow.

Example

Mario walked back and forth at the end of the pool. He had been practicing his starts for months, and today he would have a chance to show off what he had learned. Just then Dave walked into the building. Mario felt a lump in his throat. Dave was the one person he would have a hard time beating.

A. What is the main idea of this story?

- (A) Mario has been practicing jumping into the pool.
- (B) Mario is nervous about beating Dave in the swimming race.
- (C) Dave is just as good at swimming as Mario.
- (D) Mario is a good swimmer.

 **Clue** Skim the passage again after you have read it. Then read the questions. You don't have to reread the story to answer each question.

● Practice

Thousands of immigrants arrived each day at Ellis Island in New York. This was one of the reception centers set up by the United States government. The immigrants arrived with high hopes. Many had a great deal to offer the United States. However, not all those who came through Ellis Island were allowed to stay in this country.

Immigrants had forms to fill out, questions to answer, and medical exams to face. They waited for many hours in the Great Hall to hear their names called. Many had spent months in poor conditions on ships to come to the United States to make a better life. They had spent their savings to make the trip. Even after this, some were turned away.

1. What is the main idea of paragraph 1?

- (A) Thousands of immigrants arrived each day at Ellis Island.
- (B) Many immigrants were not allowed to stay in the United States.
- (C) Immigrants to the United States arrived at Ellis Island in New York.
- (D) Many immigrants arrived in the United States at Ellis Island, but not all were allowed to stay.

2. What is the main idea of paragraph 2?

- (F) Many immigrants had to go through a lot to get into the United States, and some did not make it.
- (G) Immigrants had to stand in long lines.
- (H) Many immigrants were poor.
- (J) Immigrants stood in the Great Hall waiting for their names to be called.

STOP

READING: READING COMPREHENSION

● Lesson 8: Recalling Details/Sequencing

Directions: Read the passage. Choose the best answer to the questions that follow.

Example

A medal was given to Mrs. Garcia for bravery. While going shopping, Mrs. Garcia had seen a house on fire. She could hear someone screaming. Mrs. Garcia rushed into the house even though it was on fire and full of smoke. A few minutes later, she came out carrying a young boy.

A. How did Mrs. Garcia know there was someone inside the house?

- Ⓐ She knew he was always at home.
- Ⓑ Someone told her.
- Ⓒ She saw him.
- Ⓓ She could hear him screaming.

 Clue Read the question and all the answer choices. Once you have decided on the correct answer, ask yourself, "Does this really answer the question being asked?"

● Practice

People around the world use energy every day, and some forms of energy are being used up very quickly. But resources like energy from the sun, energy from ocean waves, and hydroelectric power do not get used up completely. These resources last and last. They are called *renewable resources. Hydropower* is a renewable resource that is very common. The beginning of this word, *hydro,* refers to water. So hydropower refers to power that comes from water.

What makes hydropower work? A dam, which looks like a tall cement wall built across a body of water, raises the level of water in an area by blocking it. This causes the water to fall over the side of the dam. The falling water pushes against a machine called a *turbine.* The force of the falling water makes the blades inside spin. A machine called a *generator* captures the power from the spinning turbines. This makes electrical energy and sends out electricity to people who need it.

1. Resources that last a long time are called —

- Ⓐ hydropower.
- Ⓑ energy.
- Ⓒ fossil fuels.
- Ⓓ renewable resources.

2. What happens after the water falls over the side of the dam?

- Ⓕ The dam blocks the water in.
- Ⓖ The force makes the blades spin.
- Ⓗ The water pushes against the turbine.
- Ⓙ A generator captures the power.

3. What produces the electrical energy from the water?

- Ⓐ generator
- Ⓑ turbine
- Ⓒ dam
- Ⓓ ocean waves

 STOP

READING: READING COMPREHENSION

● Lesson 9: Inferencing/Drawing Conclusions

Directions: Read the passage. Choose the best answer to the questions that follow.

Example

Sometimes we see sand dunes near the water. These sand dunes do not always stay in the same place. The wind blows them along. Some sand dunes move only a few feet each year. Others move over 200 feet in a year.

A. Sand dunes move the most —

- (A) near the water.
- (B) where it is coldest.
- (C) where it is windiest.
- (D) where there are a lot of people.

 Clue After you read the story, think about why things happened and about what might happen after the end of the story.

● Practice

It's as black as ink out here in the pasture, and I'm as tired as an old shoe. But even if I were in my bed, I don't think I'd be sleeping like a baby tonight.

Last summer for my birthday, my parents gave me my dream horse. Her name is Goldie. She is a beautiful palomino. I love to watch her gallop around the pasture. She runs like the wind and looks so carefree. I hope I'll see her run that way again.

Yesterday, after I fed her, I forgot to close the door to the feed shed. She got into the grain and ate like a pig, which is very unhealthy for a horse. The veterinarian said I have to watch her like a hawk tonight to be sure she doesn't get colic. That's a very bad stomachache. Because he also said I should keep her moving, I have walked her around and around the pasture until I feel like we're on a merry-go-round.

Now the sun is finally beginning to peek over the horizon, and Goldie seems content. I think she's going to be as good as new.

1. **What will the narrator most likely do the next time she feeds the horse?**
   - (A) She will feed the horse too much.
   - (B) She will make sure she closes the feed shed door.
   - (C) She will give the horse plenty of water.
   - (D) She will leave the feed shed open.

2. **How much experience do you think the narrator has with horses?**
   - (F) Lots. She's probably owned many horses before.
   - (G) This is probably her first horse. She doesn't have a lot of experience.
   - (H) She's probably owned a horse before this, but not many.
   - (J) I can't tell from the story.

 STOP

READING: READING COMPREHENSION

● **Lesson 10: Fact & Opinion/Cause & Effect**

Directions: Read the passage. Choose the best answer to the questions that follow.

Example

The Hindenburg was an airship that was 804 feet (245 m) long. Airships are much more interesting than boats. Airships fly in the sky. In 1937 the Hindenburg was starting to land but blew up, killing and injuring many people.

A. Which states an opinion?

- Ⓐ Airships fly in the sky.
- Ⓑ The Hindenburg blew up, killing and injuring many people.
- Ⓒ The Hindenburg was an airship that was 804 feet (245 m) long.
- Ⓓ Airships are much more interesting than boats.

 Clue Facts are pieces of information you can prove. Opinions are what people think about things. To see if something is a fact, think about whether or not you could prove it.

● **Practice**

During the 1770s, America worked to gain independence from the British. Many struggles happened as a result.

The British passed a law in 1765 that required legal papers and other items to have a tax stamp. It was called the Stamp Act. Colonists were forced to pay a fee for the stamp. Secret groups began to work against the requirement of the tax stamp. The law was finally taken away in 1766.

In 1767, the British passed the Townshend Acts. These acts forced people to pay fees for many items, such as tea, paper, glass, lead, and paint. This wasn't fair.

Colonists were furious. On December 16, 1773, they tossed 342 chests of tea over the sides of ships in Boston Harbor. This was later called the Boston tea party. Colonists had shown that they would not accept these laws.

1. Which of the following sentences from the story states an opinion?

- Ⓐ The British passed a law in 1765 that required legal papers and other items to have a tax stamp.
- Ⓑ The law was finally taken away in 1766.
- Ⓒ This was later called the Boston tea party.
- Ⓓ This wasn't fair.

2. What caused the colonists to throw 342 chests of tea into Boston Harbor?

- Ⓕ They were angry about the Townshend Acts.
- Ⓖ They wanted to make a big pot of tea.
- Ⓗ The tea was bad.
- Ⓙ They were angry because of the Stamp Act.

 STOP

READING: READING COMPREHENSION

● Lesson 11: Parts of a Story

Directions: Read the passage. Choose the best answer to the question(s) that follows.

Example

Maggie and Isabel went to the park on Saturday. They both headed for the slides. But, they couldn't decide who should go first. Isabel said she should because she was older. Maggie said she should because Isabel always got to. Just then, Brett came over and said, "Why don't you each get on one slide and start down at the same time?"

And that's just what they did.

A. What is the turning point of this story?

- Ⓐ Maggie and Isabel argue over the slide.
- Ⓑ Brett comes up with a great solution.
- Ⓒ The girls go down the slides at the same time.
- Ⓓ The girls immediately head for the slides.

 Clue Look for the who, what, where, when, why, and how of the story.

● Practice

Joel's hockey team had been playing well all season, and this was their chance to win the tournament. He was their best player.

He glanced around at his teammates. "Guys," he said. "Let's skate really hard and show them how great we are!"

The team cheered and started to walk out to the ice. Joel turned around to grab his helmet, but it wasn't there. He looked under the benches and in the lockers, but his helmet wasn't anywhere. He sat down and felt his throat get tight. If he didn't have a helmet, he couldn't play.

Just then there was a knock on the door. Joel's mom peeked her head around the locker room door. "Thank goodness," she said. "I got here just in time with your helmet."

1. This story takes place in —

- Ⓐ a locker room.
- Ⓑ an ice center lobby.
- Ⓒ a sporting goods store.
- Ⓓ an outdoor playing field.

2. Why does Joel become upset?

- Ⓕ He can't find his hockey helmet.
- Ⓖ He missed his game.
- Ⓗ His mom will miss the game.
- Ⓙ His coach is counting on him.

3. Joel's mom resolves the conflict by —

- Ⓐ taking him out for pizza.
- Ⓑ finding his hockey stick.
- Ⓒ playing for him.
- Ⓓ bringing him his helmet.

 STOP

READING: READING COMPREHENSION

● Lesson 12: Fiction

Directions: Read the passage. Choose the best answer to the questions that follow.

Example

Bobby saw Dad lying on the sofa. He looked peaceful with his eyes closed and his hands resting on his stomach. Bobby took his roller skates and quietly left the room. A few minutes later, Bobby's mother asked where Bobby was. His dad said that Bobby had gone roller skating.

A. **How did Bobby's dad know where he was?**

(A) He has ESP.

(B) He had set up a video camera to watch him.

(C) He wasn't really asleep on the couch.

(D) Bobby left a note for him.

 Clue **Read carefully. Make sure you know all the characters and the main events. Skim or read again if necessary.**

● Practice

Brian went zooming to the park to meet his buddies for an afternoon of hoops. It would have been a perfect day, but he had to drag his little brother Pete along.

"Wait for me, Brian," whined Pete.

Brian walked Pete over to a nearby tree, handed him his lunch, and said, "Sit here and eat. Don't move until I come back and get you." Brian ran off to meet his buddies.

As Pete began eating, he heard the pitter-patter of rain falling around him. When Pete saw lightning, he ran for shelter. Suddenly a loud crack of lightning sounded. Looking behind him, Pete saw the top of the tree come crashing down right where he had been sitting. Brian saw it too, from the other side of the park.

"Pete!" Brian screamed as he ran. At the moment the lightning struck, Brian thought, "Pete's not the drag I always thought he was."

1. **What is the main conflict in this story?**

(A) Brian has to drag his brother along to the park.

(B) There is a lightning storm.

(C) The tree crashes down.

(D) Brian thinks Pete is hurt.

2. **What is Brian going to the park to play?**

(F) baseball

(G) tennis

(H) basketball

(J) soccer

3. **Why does Brian realize that Pete is not such a drag?**

(A) They have fun together.

(B) He didn't have to save him.

(C) Pete turns out to be a great runner.

(D) He realizes that he had been taking his little brother for granted.

STOP

READING: READING COMPREHENSION

● Lesson 13: Fiction

Directions: Read the passage. Choose the best answer to the questions that follow.

Example

"Please go to the store for me," said Mother. "I need a gallon of milk. Your aunt Jane is coming for supper, and I want to be sure to have enough of everything." Billy grabbed his umbrella and hurried to the store. He was glad to help because his aunt Jane was coming.

A.   Why do you think Billy is glad to help?

- (A) He thinks his mother will give him money.
- (B) He loves to go to the store.
- (C) He likes his aunt Jane.
- (D) He likes to help his mother cook.

 Clue Read carefully. Make sure you know all the characters and the main events. Skim or read again if necessary.

● Practice

"Cassie, you don't realize how grateful we are! We were afraid we wouldn't be able to get a babysitter. Here's a list of instructions. Bye, Bart," Mr. and Mrs. Bradford both said as they left.

Cassie read the note. She was supposed to feed Bart spaghetti, give him a bath, put on his pajamas, play a game with him, and then put him to bed.

But it wasn't that simple. When Bart didn't want to eat his spaghetti, he dumped it on her head. When she tried to give him a bath, he dumped the whole bottle of bubble bath in the tub. And when they tried to play a game, Bart threw blocks all over his room.

Just as Cassie was starting to relax after getting Bart in bed and cleaning up his messes, the Bradfords came home.

"The house looks great!" said Mrs. Bradford. "By the way, we would like to know if you can come back again tomorrow."

1.   What is the main problem in this story?

- (A) Bart is misbehaving.
- (B) Cassie has to clean up a mess.
- (C) The Bradfords have gone out to dinner.
- (D) Cassie does not want to babysit again.

2.   What do you think Cassie will do if the Bradfords ask her to babysit again?

- (F) She will do it.
- (G) She will find a way to get out of it.
- (H) She will volunteer eagerly.
- (J) She will offer to do it only if she doesn't have to feed Bart.

3.   What did Bart do with his spaghetti?

- (A) He threw it in the tub.
- (B) He ate it.
- (C) He dumped it on Cassie's head.
- (D) He threw it around his room.

READING: READING COMPREHENSION

● Lesson 14: Fiction

Directions: Read the passage. Choose the best answer to the questions that follow.

Example

Chandra was eating her lunch when she heard a desperate meow. She ran to the backyard to see what was wrong. Her white kitten, Darva, was up on a branch and couldn't get down. Chandra looked around the yard. She saw a ladder leaning against the shed.

A. **What will Chandra most likely do?**

- (A) She will use the ladder to rescue the kitten.
- (B) She will go back inside and finish her lunch.
- (C) She will jump up to reach the kitten.
- (D) She will lure the kitten down with a treat.

Clue Skim the passage, then read the questions. Refer back to the passage to find the answers. You don't have to reread the story for each question.

● Practice

Waterland

"Hurray!" cried Meghan. "Today is the day we're going to Waterland!" It was a hot July day, and Meghan's mom was taking her to cool off on the water slides. Meghan's new friend, Jake, was going, too.

Just then, Meghan's mom came out of her bedroom. She did not look very happy. "What's the matter, Mom? Are you afraid to get wet?" Meghan teased. "I'll bet you'll melt, just like the Wicked Witch of the West!"

Mrs. Millett didn't laugh at the joke. Instead, she told the kids that she wasn't felling well. She was too tired to drive to the water park.

Meghan and Jake were disappointed. "My mom has chronic fatigue syndrome," Meghan explained. "Her illness makes her really tired. She's still a great mom."

"Thank you, dear," said Mrs. Millett. "I'm too tired to drive, but I have an idea. You can make your own Waterland and I'll rest in the lawn chair."

Meghan and Jake set up three different sprinklers. They dragged the play slide over to the wading pool and aimed the sprinkler on the slide. Meghan and Jake got soaking wet. Mrs. Millett sat in a lawn chair and rested. The kids played all day.

"Thank you for being so understanding," Meghan's mom said. "Now I feel better, but I'm really hot! There's only one cure for that." She stood under the sprinkler with all her clothes on. She was drenched from head to toe.

Meghan laughed and said, "Now you have chronic wet syndrome." Mrs. Millett rewarded her daughter with a big, wet hug. It turned out to be a wonderful day after all, in the backyard waterland.

GO ON

READING: READING COMPREHENSION

● **Lesson 14: Fiction (cont.)**

1. **Which sentence best tells the main idea of this story?**

   (A) Meghan's mom has chronic fatigue syndrome.

   (B) Jake and Meghan miss out on Waterland, but they make their own water park and have fun anyway.

   (C) Jake and Meghan cannot go to Waterland.

   (D) Sprinklers make a great backyard water park.

2. **Which of the following happened after the kids dragged the slide over to the pool?**

   (F) Jake arrived at Meghan's house.

   (G) Meghan and Jake set up three sprinklers

   (H) Meghan's mom stood in the sprinkler with her clothes on.

   (J) Meghan's mom was too tired to drive.

3. **How do you think Mrs. Millett feels about not being able to take the kids to Waterland?**

   (A) She's glad that she won't have to spend her whole day with kids.

   (B) She feels sorry for herself and is glad she got out of it.

   (C) She's disappointed that she can't take them.

   (D) She's hurt and confused.

4. **Why didn't Meghan and Jake go to Waterland?**

   (F) They were too late.

   (G) They wanted to play in the sprinklers instead.

   (H) It was too hot outside.

   (J) Mrs. Millett was too tired to drive them.

5. **What is the turning point of this story?**

   (A) Meghan's mom feels better and gets wet in the sprinkler.

   (B) Meghan and Jake can't go to Waterland.

   (C) Meghan's mom gives her a wet hug.

   (D) Jake arrives at the house early.

6. **Why did the author write this story?**

   (F) to explain

   (G) to persuade

   (H) to entertain and inform

   (J) to understand

STOP

Name _____ Date _____

● **Lesson 15: Fiction**

Directions: Read the passage. Choose the best answer to the questions that follow.

Example

> Louis had a temperature of 101° F. He had a headache and an upset stomach. "You'd better go home," said Mr. Yeow. "You're too sick to stay in school. Don't worry about the math test. I'll give it to you when you're well enough to come back to school."

A. **Why did Louis have to leave school?**
- (A) He had been very bad.
- (B) He was too sick to stay.
- (C) He had a dentist appointment.
- (D) They had a half-day.

Clue Skim the passage, then read the questions. Refer back to the passage to find the answers. You don't have to reread the story for each question.

● **Practice**

Home Alone

"Are you sure you're going to be all right at home alone?" Chun's mother asked. "Yes, Mom," Chun replied, trying not to roll her eyes. "I'm old enough to stay here alone for three hours."

Chun's mom and dad were going to a barbecue that afternoon. Since kids weren't invited, Chun was staying home alone. It was the first time her parents had left her home by herself. Chun was a little nervous, but she was sure she could handle it.

"Let me give you a last-minute quiz to make sure," her dad said. Chun's father was a teacher, and he was always giving her little tests. "What happens if somebody calls and asks for your mom or me?"

"I tell them that you are busy and can't come to the phone right now," Chun said. "Then I take a message."

"What if there is a knock on the door?" asked her dad.

"I don't answer it, because I can't let anyone in anyway."

"Okay, here's a tough one." Her father looked very serious. "What if you hear ghosts in the closets?"

"Dad!" Chun giggled. "Our house isn't haunted. I'll be fine. Look, I have the phone number of the house where you'll be, so I can call if I need to. I've got the numbers for the police, the fire department, and the poison control center. I won't turn on the stove or leave the house. And, I'll double lock the doors behind you when you leave."

Chun's parents were satisfied. They hugged her goodbye and left for the afternoon. Chun sat for a few minutes and enjoyed the quiet of the empty house. Then she went to the kitchen to fix herself a snack. She opened the cupboard door. Then she jumped back, startled. There was a ghost in the cupboard! Chun laughed and laughed. Her dad had taped up a picture of a ghost. It said, "BOO! We love you!"

GO ON →

READING: READING COMPREHENSION

● Lesson 15: Fiction (cont.)

1. **Which answer shows the best summary of this story?**

- (A) Chun is staying home by herself for the first time and must remember all the important safety rules.
- (B) Chun cannot go to the barbecue with her mom and dad.
- (C) Chun's parents play a trick on her by hiding a paper ghost in the cupboard.
- (D) Chun enjoys a peaceful afternoon at home alone.

2. **What should Chun do if someone knocks at the door?**

- (F) She should answer it.
- (G) She should call her dad.
- (H) She should not answer it and not let anyone in.
- (J) She should see who it is before letting the person in.

3. **What do you think Chun will do if she spills drain cleaner and the dog accidentally licks some up?**

- (A) She will call her friend Sam to tell him.
- (B) She will call the fire department
- (C) She will do nothing.
- (D) She will call the poison control center and then her parents.

4. **Because kids are not invited to the barbecue, —**

- (F) they won't have any fun.
- (G) the parents will not go.
- (H) Chun must stay home alone.
- (J) Chun will not get any dinner.

5. **Who are the main characters in this story?**

- (A) Chun, her mom, and her dad
- (B) Chun and her friend Sam
- (C) Chun, her dad, and the dog
- (D) Chun and her dad

6. **What is the main reason Chun's dad keeps asking her questions?**

- (F) He wants to make sure she knows all the emergency phone numbers.
- (G) He wants to make sure she will be safe while they are gone.
- (H) He likes giving her quizzes.
- (J) He played a trick on her.

STOP

READING: READING COMPREHENSION

● Lesson 16: Nonfiction

Directions: Read the passage. Choose the best answer to the questions that follow.

Example

Can you picture a coin so big that you can hardly carry it? The country of Sweden had such a coin over 200 years ago. It was 2 feet long and 1 foot wide. The coin weighed 31 pounds.

A.   How long was the coin?
- Ⓐ   2 feet
- Ⓑ   1 foot
- Ⓒ   31 feet
- Ⓓ   3 feet

 Clue Skim the passage then read the questions. Refer back to the passage to find the answers. You don't have to reread the story for each question.

● Practice

Fossils are most often found in sedimentary rock. Suppose that a plant or animal died millions of years ago near a lake or an ocean. The mud and sand could cover it. Over many years, the mud and sand would harden and form sedimentary rock.

Two kinds of fossils in sedimentary rock are *cast* and *mold*. The mold fossil is a rock with an empty space left after the creature caught in the sediment wore away.

The cast fossil looks like a mold fossil that has been filled. Solid matter from the ground fills the empty space.

Suppose that a dinosaur stepped into soft ground and made a footprint. This would not be a cast or mold fossil. Those come from what is left of plants and creatures when they die. If a dinosaur made a footprint and walked away, the creature would not be there anymore. If the footprint hardened into rock and a scientist found it millions of years later, he would be looking at a *trace fossil*.

1.   Why does a cast fossil look like a filled mold?
- Ⓐ   The animal leaves a footprint in the dirt.
- Ⓑ   Scientists fill the empty space with plaster after they find it.
- Ⓒ   Solid matter from the ground fills the empty space left by the animal.
- Ⓓ   The fossil was found in sedimentary rock.

2.   In what kind of rock are most fossils found?
- Ⓕ   sedimentary
- Ⓖ   metamorphic
- Ⓗ   cast
- Ⓙ   mold

3.   What is the best title for this passage?
- Ⓐ   Fossil Rocks
- Ⓑ   Trace Fossils
- Ⓒ   Cast Fossils
- Ⓓ   Dinosaur Footprints

READING: READING COMPREHENSION

● **Lesson 17: Nonfiction**

Directions: Read the passage. Choose the best answer to the questions that follow.

Example

Bloodhounds are dogs that have a very good sense of smell. They are used by the police to track down people. Bloodhounds have long ears that hang down. They have wrinkled faces. Most bloodhounds are black and tan.

A. Which of the following is an opinion?

- (A) Bloodhounds have long ears.
- (B) Bloodhounds are used by the police.
- (C) Bloodhounds are good dogs to have around.
- (D) Bloodhounds have a special sense of smell.

 Clue Read carefully. Make sure you look at all the answer choices before you choose the one you think is correct.

● **Practice**

Have you ever wondered how the Great Lakes came to be? The same elements came together to create Lake Superior, Lake Michigan, Lake Huron, Lake Erie, and Lake Ontario.

Thousands of years ago, *glaciers*—huge masses of slowly moving ice—covered the earth. More and more snow fell. Temperatures grew colder. Glaciers grew larger and larger.

The movement of glaciers pulled up huge amounts of soil and rocks. These were shoved ahead and to the sides of the glaciers.

Warming temperatures caused the glaciers to melt. The glaciers had taken up space. The soil and rocks that were pulled up and shoved along by the glaciers had taken up space. When the glaciers melted, there were huge holes.

Water from the melting glaciers and from rain filled these huge holes. They were no longer holes. They were lakes!

1. **What is the best title for this passage?**
   - (A) Glaciers and Lakes
   - (B) Glaciers Take Up Space
   - (C) Melting Glaciers
   - (D) How the Great Lakes Came to Be

2. **What caused the glaciers to grow larger?**
   - (F) They pulled up huge amounts of soil and rocks.
   - (G) More snow fell and temperatures got colder.
   - (H) Temperatures grew warmer.
   - (J) Melting water fell on them.

3. **From where did the water come that filled up the glacier holes?**
   - (A) Native Americans filled up the holes to use them as lakes.
   - (B) It rained a lot.
   - (C) Rivers nearby flowed into the holes.
   - (D) It came from the melting glaciers and rain.

 STOP

READING: READING COMPREHENSION

● **Lesson 18: Nonfiction**

Directions: Read the passage. Choose the best answer to the questions that follow.

Example

How can a woodpecker bang its head into a tree all day without knocking itself out? Scientists have discovered that the bird's brain is packed inside thick, spongelike bone. Around the bone are muscles that soften the shock of the constant pecking that the bird does with its bill.

A. **Why does the woodpecker have a spongelike layer around its brain?**

(A) to soak up extra liquid in the brain

(B) to transfer messages to the rest of the body

(C) to give its head a rounded shape

(D) to protect the brain from being hurt while the bird is pecking

After you read, try to summarize the main points of the story in your head. Understanding the main points will help you recall the details.

● **Practice**

Forests and Animal Homes

Both rain forests and kelp forests are important to our ecology because they keep animals safe by providing animal homes. Rain forests keep land animals safe, while kelp forests keep sea creatures safe.

Like rain forests, kelp forests are homes for many types of animals. Crab, eel, lobster, and seahorses are just a few of the sea creatures that live in sea kelp. In California alone, kelp forests are home to more than 770 animal species. A sandy ocean bottom can make a home for some creatures, but a kelp forest can make a home for thousands more. Why? The animals can live on the many kinds of kelp surfaces—rocky and leafy ones, for example.

Like a rain forest, a kelp forest has layers. You will find three main layers in a kelp forest. They are the canopy, middle, and floor layers. The canopy is at the top, and the floor is at the bottom.

You will find different sea creatures and plants at different kelp forest levels. Herring and mackerel like to swim through the canopy, as do blue-rayed limpets. Sea slugs and snails feast on sea mats they find in the canopy.

Sea urchins look for food in the middle layer. Red seaweeds are often found in this layer of kelp forest as well, though they might be found at other levels.

Sea anemones, crabs, and lobsters live on the floor level. Older blue-rayed limpets feast here, too.

Like a rain forest, a kelp forest is a complex habitat for many sea creatures. It keeps them safe from predators and from people. And like a rain forest, to keep kelp forests an important part of our ecology, we must protect them from pollution and destruction.

GO ON

READING: READING COMPREHENSION

● Lesson 18: Nonfiction (cont.)

1. **Which sentence below best describes the main idea of this passage?**

   (A) A kelp forest has three levels.

   (B) Like rain forests, kelp forests help our ecology by providing homes for many animals.

   (C) Many sea creatures live in kelp forests and rain forests.

   (D) Kelp forests are like rain forests.

2. **Which of the following sea creatures live on the kelp forest floor?**

   (F) crabs

   (G) herring

   (H) mackerel

   (J) sea urchins

3. **Which of the following is a logical conclusion to make after reading this passage?**

   (A) Many of the animals in the kelp forests are enemies because they have to compete for food.

   (B) Kelp forests are dangerous places to visit.

   (C) Kelp forests provide many different kinds of food for sea creatures.

   (D) Kelp forests have not been studied very much by scientists.

4. **Why is a kelp forest a great home for so many animals?**

   (F) A kelp forest has many layers in which many different kinds of animals can live safely.

   (G) It is extremely large and can hold lots of animals.

   (H) The animals have been driven out of other parts of the ocean.

   (J) There is no other place for all the sea creatures to live.

5. **Which sentence below is most likely the topic sentence for this passage?**

   (A) In California alone, kelp forests are home to more than 770 animal species.

   (B) Like a rain forest, a kelp forest has layers.

   (C) Both rain forests and kelp forests are important as animal homes.

   (D) Like rain forests, kelp forests should be protected.

6. **How are rain forests and kelp forests different?**

   (F) Rain forests have animals, and kelp forests don't.

   (G) Rain forests are on land, and kelp forests are in the sea.

   (H) Kelp forests have many layers, and rain forests don't.

   (J) Rain forests are very important to our ecology, while kelp forests don't really affect it.

READING: READING COMPREHENSION

● Lesson 19: Nonfiction

Directions: Read the passage. Choose the best answer to the questions that follow.

Example

The great auk once lived on islands in the Atlantic Ocean. This large black-and-white bird had a big bill. It was an excellent swimmer and diver but couldn't fly because of its very small wings. Sailors killed these birds by the thousands. The last great auk was seen in 1844.

A. **Which of the following about the great auk is true?**

- Ⓐ It had a very small bill.
- Ⓑ It was an excellent swimmer.
- Ⓒ It had very large wings.
- Ⓓ Thousands of these birds currently live on islands in the Atlantic.

 Clue Pay close attention to the first sentences of each paragraph. These should tell you what you will read about in the rest of the paragraph.

● Practice

Alexander Graham Bell

Many believe that Alexander Graham Bell's greatest and most important personal goal was to invent the telephone, but this was not the case. Bell, who was born in 1847, called himself "a teacher of the deaf."

Bell's father was a well-known speech teacher. Bell also taught speech. He used what he had learned from his father to teach at a school for the deaf in England.

Bell went with his family to Canada in 1870. After two years, he opened a school for the deaf in Massachusetts.

The idea for the telephone came to Bell in 1874. At the same time Bell was experimenting with the telephone, he was working on equipment to help the deaf.

It was 1876 before Bell uttered the first sentence over the telephone, the well-known words: "Mr. Watson, come here; I want you."

(Watson was Bell's assistant.) Bell received a patent for the telephone in the same year.

Hundreds of cases were filed against Bell in court. Many people claimed they had already thought of the telephone. But Bell did not lose his patent. He remains on record as its inventor.

The telephone was not Bell's only invention. He received 18 patents for other works and another 12 for work he had done with partners. Fourteen of the patents were for the telephone and telegraph. Others were for inventions such as the photophone, phonograph, and for different types of airplanes.

In 1888, Bell helped found the National Geographic Society. In 1890, he also began the Alexander Graham Bell Association for the Deaf. Bell passed away in August of 1922. Alexander Graham Bell is remembered as a man of many accomplishments.

GO ON

READING: READING COMPREHENSION

● Lesson 19: Nonfiction (cont.)

1. **What is the main idea of this passage?**

    Ⓐ Alexander Graham Bell wanted to prove that he could think of many inventions.

    Ⓑ Alexander Graham Bell invented the telephone.

    Ⓒ Alexander Graham Bell was a man of many achievements.

    Ⓓ Alexander Graham Bell received 30 patents in his lifetime.

2. **Which of the following did Bell also invent?**

    Ⓕ automobile

    Ⓖ light bulb

    Ⓗ television

    Ⓙ phonograph

3. **Which of the following subjects can you infer interested Bell more than others?**

    Ⓐ electricity

    Ⓑ sound

    Ⓒ light

    Ⓓ water

4. **Which of the following is not a fact about Alexander Graham Bell?**

    Ⓕ Bell passed away in August of 1922.

    Ⓖ The telephone was not Bell's only invention.

    Ⓗ Bell's father was a well-known speech teacher.

    Ⓙ Alexander Bell was a great man.

5. **Which sentence below is the concluding sentence of this passage?**

    Ⓐ Bell passed away in August of 1922.

    Ⓑ The telephone was not Bell's only invention.

    Ⓒ In 1890, he also began the Alexander Graham Bell Association for the Deaf.

    Ⓓ Alexander Graham Bell is remembered as a man of many accomplishments.

6. **What was the author's purpose in writing this article?**

    Ⓕ to inform

    Ⓖ to entertain

    Ⓗ to persuade

    Ⓙ to understand

STOP

Name _____   Date _____

READING: READING COMPREHENSION
SAMPLE TEST

● **Directions:** Read the passage. Choose the best answer to the questions that follow.

Example

The saying "You don't know your own strength" must be true. Mildred Ludwick of Hawaii saw a little girl get struck by a car. The girl became pinned under a wheel. Ludwick used all her might and lifted the 3,000-pound car off the girl. Ludwick weighed only 105 pounds.

A.   What is the main idea of this passage?

Ⓐ Extraordinary circumstances sometimes allow people to do amazing things.

Ⓑ Even small people can do really important things.

Ⓒ You should always know your own strength.

Ⓓ Always look before you cross the street.

"Welcome to the first annual Neighborhood Guinea Pig Race!" Emily announced.

Emily's guinea pig, Ruby, was entered in the first lane. Running in the second lane was Mark's guinea pig, named Woody. Amy entered her two guinea pigs. Otis was in lane three, and Macy was in lane four. While Amy and Mark got their pets ready to race, Emily was having trouble with Ruby. Ruby was sound asleep and wouldn't budge from under her wood shavings. "Come out, little piggie," Emily encouraged, but Ruby wouldn't budge.

"Why don't you try a carrot?" suggested Mark, holding out a small carrot. "That always works with Woody."

Emily poked on Ruby with the carrot and then stuck it under her nose. Sure enough, Ruby got up off her belly and followed the carrot.

"It worked!" exclaimed Emily. "Thanks, Mark!"

1.   What is the main problem in this story?

Ⓐ Emily is impatient with Ruby.

Ⓑ Ruby is lazy.

Ⓒ Ruby won't come out of her cage for the race.

Ⓓ Ruby likes carrots too much.

2.   What are the names of Amy's two guinea pigs?

Ⓕ Milo and Otis

Ⓖ Ruby and Woody

Ⓗ Woody and Otis

Ⓙ Otis and Macy

3.   Why does Ruby finally budge?

Ⓐ Emily lures her out with a carrot.

Ⓑ The race is about to start.

Ⓒ She wakes up.

Ⓓ Mark uses Woody to get her to come out.

GO ON

READING: READING COMPREHENSION
SAMPLE TEST (cont.)

Read the passage. Choose the best answer to the questions that follow.

Earth and Venus are alike in many ways.

Earth and Venus are both planets that have volcanoes. Venus has more volcanoes than any other planet. Scientists have mapped more than 1,600 on Venus. Some scientists believe that there may be more than one million volcanoes on the planet.

Both planets look the same. They both have clouds and a thick atmosphere. The two are almost the same size and have almost the same mass. Venus's orbit around the sun is much like Earth's.

Though Earth and Venus are alike, there are also some differences. Water does not exist on Venus. The temperature on Venus is much hotter than on Earth.

On Earth, volcanoes erupt in a number of different ways. On Venus, however, almost all volcanoes erupt with flat lava flows. Scientists have not found information to show that any of Venus's volcanoes erupt and spew great amounts of ash into the sky.

4. **What is the topic sentence of this passage?**
    - (F) Both planets look the same.
    - (G) Though Earth and Venus are alike, there are also some differences.
    - (H) Earth and Venus are both planets that have volcanoes.
    - (J) Earth and Venus are alike in many ways.

5. **How is Venus's climate different than Earth's?**
    - (A) Venus gets more rain.
    - (B) Earth has more hot days during the year than Venus.
    - (C) The temperature on Venus is much hotter than on Earth.
    - (D) Venus has more cloudy days than Earth.

6. **Which of the following states a fact about Earth and/or Venus?**
    - (F) Water does not exist on Venus.
    - (G) It might be nice to visit Venus.
    - (H) Some people think Earth looks like Venus.
    - (J) It would be the same to live on Venus as it is here.

GO ON

READING: READING COMPREHENSION
SAMPLE TEST (cont.)

● **Directions:** Read the passage. Choose the best answer to each question on the next page.

Missing Super-Cool

Lizzy loved to play with her Super-Cool dolls. She had Twirly-Curl Shirl, Beach Ball Belinda, and Can-Crushing Cal. Lizzy loved to dress them up and pretend they were driving the car or going to the ice cream shop. They had a big plastic house they lived in, a purple car that really drove, and a beauty parlor where they could get their hair done.

Lizzy played make-believe all the time. Sometimes she would put all her Super-Cool dolls and their stuff in a suitcase and carry it across the driveway to her friend Tait's house. They would play with their dolls together for hours and hours. Sometimes they would even play with the dolls outside.

One day, Lizzy was getting out her dolls to play at home and noticed that some of Twirly-Curl Shirl's barrettes were missing. "That's funny," she thought. "I guess I must have lost them."

The next week, when Lizzy was playing at home again, she noticed that Beach Ball Belinda's sunglasses and flip-flops were missing. "Something's going on here," Lizzy thought.

The next day, Lizzy was playing at Tait's house again. When Tait left the room to go to the bathroom, Lizzy was picking through Tait's box of Super-Cool clothes. She was moving some clothes aside when she noticed her missing barrettes at the bottom of the box. She gasped and picked them out. She sorted through the box some more and found the

missing sunglasses and flip-flops. "Oh, my gosh," she said.

Lizzy didn't know what to do. Should she ask Tait if she had taken them? But how else could they have gotten there? She didn't want to get in a fight with her best friend, but she didn't want Tait to steal from her again. She didn't know what she should do, so she decided to go and ask her mom.

That night when she was helping her mom set the table, Lizzy asked her mom about it. Her mom thought for a few seconds. "I think you should ask Tait if you left anything over there. Tell her that you found something there last time and wondered if you left anything again. That way you can give her the chance to confess if she wants."

The next day Lizzy did just as her mom had suggested.

"Well," said Tait, "My mom won't let me get those dolls, and their clothes are so cool. I took those things because I just love them. I'm sorry I did, but I just wanted to play with them."

"That's okay, Tait, I'll let you play with my stuff while I'm over here, but it has to go back home with me, okay?"

"Okay. Let's play right now."

GO ON

READING: READING COMPREHENSION
SAMPLE TEST (cont.)

7. **What is the main message of this story?**

   (A) If you really want something, just take it.

   (B) You should always be honest with your friends.

   (C) Playing nicely is the only way to play.

   (D) Super-Cool dolls are better played with at your own house.

8. **To which Super-Cool doll do the missing barrettes belong?**

   (F) Can-Crushing Cal

   (G) Beach Ball Belinda

   (H) Twirly-Curl Shirl

   (J) All of the above

9. **How do you think Lizzy would have felt if Tait hadn't said anything about stealing the toys?**

   (A) Sad; she may have felt that she couldn't trust Tait.

   (B) Happy; she'd be grateful that she wouldn't have to talk about it.

   (C) Jealous; she would want to play at her house instead.

   (D) Calm; she would ask her mother to buy her another one.

10. **Because Tait couldn't have the toys she wanted —**

    (F) she took them from Lizzy.

    (G) she threw a temper tantrum.

    (H) she got other ones.

    (J) she played with her own.

11. **Who are the characters in this story?**

    (A) Shirl, Belinda, and Cal

    (B) Lizzy and Tait

    (C) Lizzy, Tait, and Mom

    (D) Lizzy, Tait, and Shirl

GO ON

READING: READING COMPREHENSION
SAMPLE TEST (cont.)

● **Directions:** Read the passage. Choose the best answer to each question on the next page.

The Underground Railroad

The Underground Railroad was a group of people who helped slaves escape to freedom. Those in charge of the escape effort were often called *conductors*, just like the conductors of a train. The people escaping were known as *passengers*, just like train passengers. And the places where the escaping slaves stopped for help were often called *stations*, just like the places trains stop.

Like a train ride, the Underground Railroad moved people along, but the way in which they moved was very different from a train ride. Those who escaped often followed routes that had been laid out by others before them. However, unlike a train ride, some routes went underground through dirt tunnels without any sort of tracks.

Similar to a train ride, those traveling the Underground Railroad often traveled great distances, but they had no train seats and no gentle rocking of the train car on the tracks. Instead, they had difficult trails to follow. They rarely traveled during the day, finding that it was safer to travel at night.

Escaping slaves had to be certain that they could find their way. They needed food and water to make the journey. Conductors often helped with this. One of the most famous Underground Railroad conductors was Harriet Tubman. She had escaped slavery herself. Another famous conductor was Levi Coffin.

Experts disagree about how well the Underground Railroad was organized. Still, it is believed that the system helped thousands of slaves reach freedom between 1830 and 1860.

GO ON

12. **What's is the author's purpose in writing this article?**

   (F) to quiz us on train vocabulary

   (G) to tell us about how the Underground Railroad worked

   (H) to tell a story about Harriet Tubman

   (J) to explain the meaning of the name *Underground Railroad*

13. **What were people called who were in charge of groups of escaping slaves?**

   (A) conductors

   (B) stations

   (C) passengers

   (D) masters

14. **What two emotions below best describe how slaves traveling on the Underground Railroad might have felt?**

   (F) frightened and excited

   (G) disappointed and mad

   (H) carefree and happy

   (J) silly and lighthearted

15. **Because of the Underground Railroad —**

   (A) other programs like it were set up.

   (B) many people had jobs.

   (C) conductors had to be found to run it.

   (D) thousands of slaves escaped.

16. **Which of the following is not a supporting detail for the article?**

   (F) The Underground Railroad was a group of people who helped slaves escape to freedom.

   (G) Still, it is believed that the system helped thousands of slaves reach freedom between 1830 and 1860.

   (H) The people escaping were known as *passengers*, just like train passengers.

   (J) The Underground Railroad offered free train rides to people.

17. **Which of the following is *not* a way in which the Underground Railroad and trains are alike?**

   (A) They have passengers.

   (B) They travel great distances.

   (C) They stop at stations.

   (D) They travel on tracks.

ANSWER SHEET

STUDENT'S NAME

LAST	FIRST	MI

(Bubble grid A–Z for each letter column)

SCHOOL

TEACHER

FEMALE ◯   MALE ◯

BIRTH DATE

MONTH	DAY	YEAR

JAN ◯
FEB ◯
MAR ◯
APR ◯
MAY ◯
JUN ◯
JUL ◯
AUG ◯
SEP ◯
OCT ◯
NOV ◯
DEC ◯

DAY: (0)(0) (1)(1) (2)(2) (3)(3) (4) (5) (6) (7) (8) (9)

YEAR: (0)(1)(2)(3)(4)(5)(5)(6)(6)(7)(7)(8)(8)(9)(9)(0)

GRADE
③ ④ ⑤

Part 1: VOCABULARY

A Ⓐ Ⓑ Ⓒ Ⓓ	**6** Ⓕ Ⓖ Ⓗ Ⓙ	**13** Ⓐ Ⓑ Ⓒ Ⓓ	**20** Ⓕ Ⓖ Ⓗ Ⓙ	**27** Ⓐ Ⓑ Ⓒ Ⓓ
B Ⓕ Ⓖ Ⓗ Ⓙ	**7** Ⓐ Ⓑ Ⓒ Ⓓ	**14** Ⓕ Ⓖ Ⓗ Ⓙ	**21** Ⓐ Ⓑ Ⓒ Ⓓ	**28** Ⓕ Ⓖ Ⓗ Ⓙ
1 Ⓐ Ⓑ Ⓒ Ⓓ	**8** Ⓕ Ⓖ Ⓗ Ⓙ	**15** Ⓐ Ⓑ Ⓒ Ⓓ	**22** Ⓕ Ⓖ Ⓗ Ⓙ	**29** Ⓐ Ⓑ Ⓒ Ⓓ
2 Ⓕ Ⓖ Ⓗ Ⓙ	**9** Ⓐ Ⓑ Ⓒ Ⓓ	**16** Ⓕ Ⓖ Ⓗ Ⓙ	**23** Ⓐ Ⓑ Ⓒ Ⓓ	**30** Ⓕ Ⓖ Ⓗ Ⓙ
3 Ⓐ Ⓑ Ⓒ Ⓓ	**10** Ⓕ Ⓖ Ⓗ Ⓙ	**17** Ⓐ Ⓑ Ⓒ Ⓓ	**24** Ⓕ Ⓖ Ⓗ Ⓙ	**31** Ⓐ Ⓑ Ⓒ Ⓓ
4 Ⓕ Ⓖ Ⓗ Ⓙ	**11** Ⓐ Ⓑ Ⓒ Ⓓ	**18** Ⓕ Ⓖ Ⓗ Ⓙ	**25** Ⓐ Ⓑ Ⓒ Ⓓ	**32** Ⓕ Ⓖ Ⓗ Ⓙ
5 Ⓐ Ⓑ Ⓒ Ⓓ	**12** Ⓕ Ⓖ Ⓗ Ⓙ	**19** Ⓐ Ⓑ Ⓒ Ⓓ	**26** Ⓕ Ⓖ Ⓗ Ⓙ	**33** Ⓐ Ⓑ Ⓒ Ⓓ

Part 2: FICTION

A Ⓐ Ⓑ Ⓒ Ⓓ	**7** Ⓐ Ⓑ Ⓒ Ⓓ
1 Ⓐ Ⓑ Ⓒ Ⓓ	**8** Ⓕ Ⓖ Ⓗ Ⓙ
2 Ⓕ Ⓖ Ⓗ Ⓙ	**9** Ⓐ Ⓑ Ⓒ Ⓓ
3 Ⓐ Ⓑ Ⓒ Ⓓ	**10** Ⓕ Ⓖ Ⓗ Ⓙ
4 Ⓕ Ⓖ Ⓗ Ⓙ	**11** Ⓐ Ⓑ Ⓒ Ⓓ
5 Ⓐ Ⓑ Ⓒ Ⓓ	**12** Ⓕ Ⓖ Ⓗ Ⓙ
6 Ⓕ Ⓖ Ⓗ Ⓙ	

Part 3: NONFICTION

A Ⓐ Ⓑ Ⓒ Ⓓ	**7** Ⓐ Ⓑ Ⓒ Ⓓ	**14** Ⓕ Ⓖ Ⓗ Ⓙ
1 Ⓐ Ⓑ Ⓒ Ⓓ	**8** Ⓕ Ⓖ Ⓗ Ⓙ	**15** Ⓐ Ⓑ Ⓒ Ⓓ
2 Ⓕ Ⓖ Ⓗ Ⓙ	**9** Ⓐ Ⓑ Ⓒ Ⓓ	
3 Ⓐ Ⓑ Ⓒ Ⓓ	**10** Ⓕ Ⓖ Ⓗ Ⓙ	
4 Ⓕ Ⓖ Ⓗ Ⓙ	**11** Ⓐ Ⓑ Ⓒ Ⓓ	
5 Ⓐ Ⓑ Ⓒ Ⓓ	**12** Ⓕ Ⓖ Ⓗ Ⓙ	
6 Ⓕ Ⓖ Ⓗ Ⓙ	**13** Ⓐ Ⓑ Ⓒ Ⓓ	

1-57768-974-7 Spectrum Test Practice 4

Name _____ Date_____

READING PRACTICE TEST

● **Part 1: Vocabulary**

Examples

For items A and 1–8, choose the word or words that mean the same or about the same as the underlined word.

A. <u>conceal</u> a crime
- Ⓐ commit
- Ⓑ cover up
- Ⓒ know about
- Ⓓ punish

For item B, read the question. Choose the answer you think is correct.

B. Which tree was named for Pierre Magnol, the scientist who discovered it?
- Ⓕ pine
- Ⓖ maple
- Ⓗ magnolia
- Ⓙ mahogany

---

1. <u>grab</u> a cookie
   - Ⓐ reach for
   - Ⓑ bake
   - Ⓒ eat
   - Ⓓ break

2. give a <u>signal</u>
   - Ⓕ radio
   - Ⓖ poster
   - Ⓗ gift
   - Ⓙ sign

3. <u>thorough</u> cleaning
   - Ⓐ quick
   - Ⓑ necessary
   - Ⓒ complete
   - Ⓓ house

4. <u>explore</u> the island
   - Ⓕ search
   - Ⓖ find
   - Ⓗ stalk
   - Ⓙ look for

5. To <u>consult</u> someone is to —
   - Ⓐ compliment
   - Ⓑ get advice
   - Ⓒ insult
   - Ⓓ give advice

6. If someone is <u>generous</u>, he is —
   - Ⓕ giving
   - Ⓖ guilty
   - Ⓗ selfish
   - Ⓙ greedy

7. If something is <u>spoiled</u> it is —
   - Ⓐ crusty
   - Ⓑ cooked
   - Ⓒ sunburned
   - Ⓓ ruined

8. She put her <u>cloak</u> on.
   - Ⓕ hat
   - Ⓖ cape
   - Ⓗ sweater
   - Ⓙ scarf

GO ON

READING PRACTICE TEST
Part 1: Vocabulary (cont.)

For items 9–12, choose the word or words that mean the same or about the same as the underlined word.

9. The girls <u>abandoned</u> their brothers in the woods.
   Abandoned means —
   - Ⓐ left alone intentionally
   - Ⓑ played with
   - Ⓒ amused
   - Ⓓ walked with

10. To demonstrate, Janice made a <u>circular</u> motion with her hand.
    Circular means —
    - Ⓕ circus
    - Ⓖ in a circle
    - Ⓗ waving
    - Ⓙ slapping

11. Raschel wants to <u>discontinue</u> her magazine subscription.
    To discontinue is to —
    - Ⓐ reorder
    - Ⓑ order
    - Ⓒ stop
    - Ⓓ pay for

12. My older brother went on an <u>expedition</u> to Central America to study pyramids.
    An expedition is a —
    - Ⓕ journey with a purpose
    - Ⓖ vacation
    - Ⓗ trip
    - Ⓙ stroll

For items 13–17, choose the word that means the opposite of the underlined word.

13. <u>weeping</u> child
    - Ⓐ young
    - Ⓑ laughing
    - Ⓒ skipping
    - Ⓓ sad

14. <u>dangerous</u> snake
    - Ⓕ slimy
    - Ⓖ moist
    - Ⓗ harmless
    - Ⓙ long

15. friends and <u>foes</u>
    - Ⓐ friends
    - Ⓑ enemies
    - Ⓒ pets
    - Ⓓ parents

16. <u>quality</u> foods
    - Ⓕ salty
    - Ⓖ dessert
    - Ⓗ well-made
    - Ⓙ bad

17. <u>coarse</u> salt
    - Ⓐ natural
    - Ⓑ rough
    - Ⓒ tough
    - Ⓓ fine

GO ON

Name _____ Date_____

For items 18–21, read the two sentences with blanks. Choose the word that fits best in both sentences.

18. My _____ is in the closet.
    Add a new _____ of paint.
    - (F) hat
    - (G) color
    - (H) shirt
    - (J) coat

19. **The photography _____ meets today.**
    The cave man carried a _____ .
    - (A) group
    - (B) club
    - (C) spear
    - (D) class

20. **He will need new swimming _____ .**
    Load those _____ in the van.
    - (F) goggles
    - (G) shoes
    - (H) boxes
    - (J) trunks

21. **Our teacher tells us not to _____ anyone.**
    The _____ at the party was tasty.
    - (A) food
    - (B) hit
    - (C) punch
    - (D) juice

For items 22–23, choose the answer in which the underlined word is used in the same way as the sentence in the box.

22. | The sky was clear. |
    - (F) Clear away those dinner dishes.
    - (G) The tower radioed that we were in the clear.
    - (H) He said it would be clear sailing from here on in.
    - (J) Clear skies and bright sun were forecast for today.

23. | Watch out for that falling limb. |
    - (A) Andrew checked his watch for the time.
    - (B) The captain asked him to take the first watch.
    - (C) Watch your step.
    - (D) We kept the watch fire burning all night.

For items 24–25, choose the answer that best defines the underlined part.

24. **disbelieve   disorganized**
    - (F) absence of
    - (G) more
    - (H) less than
    - (J) again

25. **gentleness   kindness**
    - (A) quality of
    - (B) less
    - (C) more
    - (D) opposite of

GO ON

READING PRACTICE TEST
Part 1: Vocabulary (cont.)

26. Which of these words probably comes from the Latin word *crimen*, meaning *accusation*?

    (F) cringe

    (G) cry

    (H) criminal

    (J) crimp

27. Which of these words probably comes from the Greek word *musterion*, meaning *secret rite*?

    (A) musky

    (B) mystic

    (C) must

    (D) muster

28. We hiked to a _____ campsite. Which word means the campsite was *far away*?

    (F) remote

    (G) pleasant

    (H) crowded

    (J) level

29. The girls were _____ to the show after they bought their tickets. Which word means that they were *allowed to enter*?

    (A) going

    (B) cast

    (C) admitted

    (D) shown

Read the paragraph. Choose the word that fits best in each numbered blank.

Mountain gorillas live in the _____(30) in Rwanda, Uganda, and the Democratic Republic of the Congo. These _____,(31) beautiful animals are becoming very rare. They have lost much of their habitat as people move in and take over their land. Although there are _____(32) laws protecting gorillas, poachers continue to hunt them. Scientists and park rangers are working hard to _____(33) the mountain gorillas.

30. (F) deserts

    (G) forests

    (H) lakes

    (J) valleys

31. (A) large

    (B) small

    (C) skinny

    (D) violent

32. (F) loose

    (G) easy

    (H) stupid

    (J) strict

33. (A) chase away

    (B) hunt

    (C) protect

    (D) kill

STOP

Name _____ Date _____

READING PRACTICE TEST

● Part 2: Fiction

Directions: Read the passage. Choose the best answer to the questions that follow.

Example

"I can't find my baseball glove," complained Jane. "I left it in the closet, but it's not there. I must use my own glove if I'm going to play my best." That afternoon, just before her baseball game, Jane said, "I feel that I'm going to win for sure."

A. **Why did Jane's attitude probably change just before the game?**

- Ⓐ She found her glove.
- Ⓑ Her whole family was there.
- Ⓒ She had been promised ice cream after the game.
- Ⓓ Her coach had given a great pep talk.

Cassie's mom has errands to run, so Cassie agrees to stay home to babysit for her little brother, who is asleep. Her mom also leaves Cassie a list of chores to do while she is gone. Cassie will be able to go to the mall with her friends when her chores are finished and her mom gets back.

As soon as Cassie's mom leaves, Cassie starts calling her friends on the phone. She talks to Kim for 20 minutes and to Beth for 15 minutes. She is supposed to call Maria when she finishes talking to Jackie.

After talking on the phone, Cassie decides to do her nails while she watches a movie on TV. After the movie, Cassie listens to the radio and reads a magazine.

Before Cassie realizes it, three and a half hours have passed and her mom is back home. Her mom walks in and finds the kitchen still a mess, crumbs all over the carpet, dusty furniture, and Cassie's little brother screaming in his room.

1. **Who was Cassie going to call after Beth?**

- Ⓐ Kim
- Ⓑ Maria
- Ⓒ Jackie
- Ⓓ her mom

2. **Which of the following is a chore Cassie probably wasn't supposed to do?**

- Ⓕ dust
- Ⓖ listen for her brother
- Ⓗ clean her room
- Ⓙ clean the kitchen

3. **What do you think the resolution to this problem will be?**

- Ⓐ Cassie's little brother will have to do all the chores.
- Ⓑ Cassie will be punished and will not go to the mall.
- Ⓒ Cassie's mom will drive her to the mall.
- Ⓓ Cassie, her mom, and her brother will watch a movie.

Read the passage. Choose the best answer to each question.

David's grandpa is coming to visit for a week. David is really excited because he and his grandpa have always had a great time together. But, David is also nervous. His grandpa had a stroke a few months ago, and David's mom said his grandpa moves a little slower than he used to. "Oh, well," thinks David, "we'll still have fun."

On the day of Grandpa's arrival, David is up early. He is too excited to sleep. Finally, it is time to go to the airport. Off the plane comes Grandpa. But, he is using a cane! Mom never told David that. What about their long walks down to the creek? David gives his grandpa a big hug. His grandpa seems really old and tired.

On the way home, Grandpa keeps talking about how he doesn't want to be in anyone's way and if David's family gets tired of him, they can send him home early. David feels sorry for his grandpa. Then David starts coming up with all kinds of new things they can do together, like build model airplanes, watch movies, put together his train set, and organize David's baseball card collection.

"No way are you going home one second early, Grandpa," says David. His grandpa looks very happy.

4. **Why is this visit different from others?**
   - F David is excited about the visit.
   - G Grandpa will not be staying as long this time.
   - H Grandma is coming along with Grandpa.
   - J Grandpa has had a stroke since that last time David saw him.

5. **How does David feel about his grandpa's visit?**
   - A exhilarated
   - B anxious
   - C optimistic
   - D depressed

6. **What is the turning point in this story?**
   - F David sees his grandpa using a cane.
   - G David's grandpa arrives.
   - H David thinks of lots of new things he can do with his grandpa.
   - J Grandpa looks very happy.

READING PRACTICE TEST
Part 2: Fiction (cont.)

Read the passage. Choose the best answer to each question on the next page.

Class President

Quinn was running for class president. He and his friend Zack hung colored posters up in the hallways. They declared, "QUINN SHOULD WIN!"

A fifth grader walked by them as they hung one on the door to the library. He read the poster and asked, "Why? Why should *you* win?" and then walked away.

Quinn had never thought about *why* before. He knew that he was popular and that a lot of people would vote for him.

"I suppose you should have some issues," Zack commented. "More recess time? Hey, how about that new gumball machine in the boys' bathroom you're always talking about?"

In the election meeting that afternoon, Mrs. Jacobs, the school principal, told them it was a great responsibility to be each class's president. All candidates running, she said, should be honest. "Let your platform speak for itself," she said.

At home, Quinn and Zack made up new campaign posters that said, "VOTE QUINN: New gumball machine in the boys' room. Everyone will play soccer at lunch. Taco day is abolished!"

The next day at school, some of Quinn's regular friends avoided him, especially the girls. When he asked J.D. if he wanted to play soccer at lunch, J.D. responded, "Of course, Your Majesty."

"What's the matter with everyone?" Quinn muttered while standing in the lunch line.

"I'll tell you what's wrong," said a small girl in line behind him. "Nobody likes your campaign promises. The girls couldn't care less if you're going to get a gumball machine in the boys' room. A lot of people like taco day. And, nobody wants to be told they have to play soccer at recess. Some people like to play other games. You only made promises about what you like."

Quinn thought about what he could do. He decided that if he wanted to know what his classmates wanted, he should take a poll. So, he and Zack asked each fourth grader what they wanted most to change in their school. They made a bar graph so they could see what was most important to fourth graders. Then Quinn and Zack made up new campaign posters. Quinn's friends started talking to him again, and the next week he won the election. Quinn realized that listening to your classmates is the most important thing a class president can do.

7. **What is the main message of this story?**

   (A) Holding a public office is an important responsibility.

   (B) School elections are very complicated.

   (C) Popularity is more important than campaign promises.

   (D) Girls and boys don't always like the same things.

8. **What was Quinn's first campaign slogan?**

   (F) New gumball machine in the boys' room.

   (G) Everyone will play soccer at lunch.

   (H) Quinn should win!

   (J) Taco day is abolished!

9. **Which of the following probably would have happened if Quinn hadn't changed his slogans?**

   (A) He would have won anyway.

   (B) Mrs. Jacobs would have told him he couldn't run.

   (C) Zack would have refused to speak to him.

   (D) He would have lost the election.

10. **What causes Quinn's friends to stop speaking to him?**

    (F) He puts up his campaign posters.

    (G) He only makes promises for things he wants.

    (H) He decides to run for class president.

    (J) He changes his campaign promises.

11. **What is the turning point in this story?**

    (A) The girl in line tells him what is wrong with his promises.

    (B) Quinn decides to ask his classmates what they want.

    (C) Quinn wins the election.

    (D) Some of Quinn's friends refuse to talk to him.

12. **Which genre is this story?**

    (F) western

    (G) mystery

    (H) drama

    (J) nonfiction

STOP

Name _____ Date _____

READING PRACTICE TEST

● **Part 3: Nonfiction**

Directions: Read the passage. Choose the best answer to each question.

Example

Before the 1800s, people didn't have right or left shoes. They had shoes of just one shape that they used for both feet. When people first saw right and left shoes, they laughed. They called them *crooked shoes*.

A. **Which of the following is an opinion?**

Ⓐ Before the 1800s, people didn't have right or left shoes.

Ⓑ People called the new shoes *crooked shoes*.

Ⓒ People had only one shape of shoe.

Ⓓ The new shoes were funny-looking.

Perhaps you have heard that many types of bats have very small eyes and do not see well. Still, as they swoop through the night, they do not bump into objects and are able to find food, even though they can't see their prey. How is this possible? Echolocation!

You might recognize the beginning of the word *echolocation* as *echo*, and you might recognize the last part of the word as *location*. This gives you clues about how echolocation works. The bat sends out sounds. The sounds bounce off objects and return to the bat. Echolocation not only tells the bat that objects are nearby, it also tells the bat just how far away the objects are.

Bats are not the only creatures that use echolocation, Porpoises and some types of whales and birds use it as well. It is a very effective tool for the animals that use it.

1. **What is the main idea of this passage?**

Ⓐ Bats cannot see very well.

Ⓑ Many animals use echolocation.

Ⓒ Echolocation is an effective tool for bats and other animals.

Ⓓ Bats are not the only creatures that use echolocation.

2. **Which two words make up the word *echolocation*?**

Ⓕ *ech* and *olocation*

Ⓖ *echolocate* and *tion*

Ⓗ *echo* and *locate*

Ⓙ *echo* and *location*

3. **Bats have to use echolocation mainly because —**

Ⓐ they have no eyes.

Ⓑ they have poor eyesight.

Ⓒ they have big ears.

Ⓓ they fly past lots of obstacles.

GO ON

READING PRACTICE TEST
Part 3: Nonfiction (cont.)

Read the passage. Choose the best answer to each question on the next page.

The Origins of the Telegraph

Have you ever watched someone tap a key and send a code for S.O.S.? Perhaps you have seen an old film and seen a ship about to sink. Perhaps someone was tapping wildly on a device, trying to send for help.

From where did this system of tapping out dashes and dots come? Who invented this electronic device? Samuel Morse invented the telegraph and the electronic alphabet called Morse code.

When Morse was young, he was an artist. People in New York knew his work well and liked it a great deal. Being well known, Morse decided to run for office. He ran for the office of New York mayor and congressman, but he lost these political races.

In 1832, while Morse was sailing back to the United States from Europe, he thought of an electronic telegraph. This would help people communicate across great distances, even from ship to shore. He was anxious to put together his invention as quickly as possible. Interestingly, someone else had also thought of this same idea.

By 1835, he had put together his first telegraph, but it was only experimental. In 1844, he built a telegraph line from Baltimore to Washington, D.C. He later made his telegraph better, and in 1849, was granted a patent by the U.S. government. Within a few years, people communicated across 23,000 miles (37,007 km) of telegraph wire.

As a result of Samuel Morse's invention, trains ran more safely. Conductors could warn about dangers or problems across great distances and ask for help. People in business could communicate more easily, which made it easier to sell their goods and services. Morse had changed communication forever.

GO ON

4. **What is the main idea of this article?**

    (F) Trains run more safely because of the telegraph.

    (G) Telegraphs send electronic signals to communicate.

    (H) By the 1850s, people communicated effectively by telegraph.

    (J) Morse's invention of the telegraph changed communication forever.

5. **Before 1832, Morse had —**

    (A) run for office in New York.

    (B) improved his telegraph.

    (C) built his first telegraph.

    (D) come up with the idea for the telegraph.

6. **Which of the following can you infer about Samuel Morse's childhood?**

    (F) He was well educated.

    (G) He had to work at a young age to support his family.

    (H) He lived on a farm and was not able to go to school.

    (J) He was abandoned at a young age and forced to live on the streets.

7. **What can you infer about long-distance communication before Morse's invention?**

    (A) It was easy.

    (B) No one was interested in it.

    (C) It was difficult to do quickly.

    (D) There was no long-distance communication.

8. **Which of the following sentences from the article concludes this reading selection?**

    (F) As a result of Samuel Morse's invention, trains ran more safely.

    (G) People in business could communicate more easily, which made it easier to sell their goods and services.

    (H) Within a few years, people communicated across 23,000 miles (37,007 km) of telegraph wire.

    (J) Morse had changed communication forever.

9. **How is the telegraph not similar to the telephone?**

    (A) helps communicate over long distances

    (B) makes people safer

    (C) helps people sell goods and services

    (D) lets people hear their loved ones' voices

GO ON

Read the passage. Choose the best answer to each question on the next page.

Radio

Inventor Guglielmo Marconi came to the United States in 1899. Telegraph communication by wire was already in place, but Marconi wanted to show off his wireless communication—radio.

Marconi's invention could send Morse code without using any wires. He thought this would help with business communication. When introducing his work, he also planned to show how his invention could do things such as broadcasting a sporting event.

Other people had more and different ideas. These ideas led to programs that included spoken words and music being broadcast on the radio. Operas, comedy hours, and important speeches were now being heard in many homes throughout the country. Two famous radio broadcasts were the "War of the Worlds" presentation on October 31, 1938, a fictional story that told about invading aliens; and President Roosevelt's radio announcement of the Japanese attack on Pearl Harbor on December 8, 1941.

In 1922, there were 30 radio stations that sent broadcasts. By 1923, the number had grown to an amazing 556! There was a problem with so many stations broadcasting, however. There was no regular way to do things. Radio station owners organized their stations any way they saw fit.

Even though stations organized into networks, broadcasting still was not organized. The United States government passed laws to regulate radio. This let station owners know which airwaves they could use. The laws also addressed what was okay to say on the radio and what was not appropriate.

Even though television and the Internet are with us today, most homes and cars have radios. It looks as though this kind of communication is here to stay, thanks to Mr. Marconi and his invention.

READING PRACTICE TEST
Part 3: Nonfiction (cont.)

10. **Which of the following would be an appropriate title for this article?**

    (F) Guglielmo Marconi

    (G) Radio: How Did It Begin?

    (H) Radio Is Here to Stay

    (J) Wireless, Here We Go!

11. **Which of the following came before there were 30 radio stations that sent broadcasts?**

    (A) There were an amazing 556 radio stations.

    (B) The "War of the Worlds" program was broadcast.

    (C) President Roosevelt announced the attack on Pearl Harbor.

    (D) Guglielmo Marconi came to the United States.

12. **What can you infer about people's reactions to radio?**

    (F) They didn't like it and preferred to watch events.

    (G) It took a long time for them to get used to the idea.

    (H) They immediately liked it and were excited about it.

    (J) They shunned Marconi and thought his invention was too modern.

13. **Which of the following is a fact?**

    (A) Radio was the most helpful invention ever created.

    (B) Mr. Marconi was a genius.

    (C) Radios send signals without wires.

    (D) Radio will never go away.

14. **Which of the following is not a supporting detail found in this article?**

    (F) The United States government passed laws to regulate radio.

    (G) Marconi won the Nobel Prize in 1909.

    (H) Marconi wanted to introduce his wireless communication.

    (J) Marconi came to the United States in 1899.

15. **Why did the author most likely write this article?**

    (A) to inform us about the introduction of radio in the United States

    (B) to prove how successful a life Marconi had

    (C) to inspire us to invent more communication devices

    (D) to inform us about all the possible radio shows there are to make

LANGUAGE: LANGUAGE MECHANICS

● Lesson 1: Punctuation

Directions: Read each sentence. Choose the punctuation mark that is needed in the sentence. If no more punctuation is needed, choose "None."

Examples

A. Do you think the film is scary

- (A) .
- (B) !
- (C) ?
- (D) None

B. "This is fun, answered Lettie.

- (F) ,
- (G) ?
- (H) "
- (J) None

Clue Look carefully at all the answer choices before you choose the one you think is correct. Make sure you completely fill in the circle for your answer choice.

● Practice

1. The clouds were dark, and the wind was getting stronger.

- (A) !
- (B) .
- (C) ?
- (D) None

2. Jody please don't forget to feed the cat.

- (F) ?
- (G) !
- (H) ,
- (J) None

3. "Your brother just called," said Kyle.

- (A) .
- (B) ,
- (C) !
- (D) None

4. Mary Lucy, and Kylie all went to the movies.

- (F) .
- (G) !
- (H) ,
- (J) None

5. "Please take out the trash" Mom said.

- (A) "
- (B) ,
- (C) .
- (D) None

6. How much money do we need

- (F) .
- (G) ,
- (H) ?
- (J) None

GO ON

LANGUAGE: LANGUAGE MECHANICS

● Lesson 1: Punctuation (cont.)

For items 7–12, choose the line that has a punctuation error. If there is no error, choose "No mistakes."

7.
  (A) A snake skeleton has many ribs
  (B) A large snake may have as
  (C) many as 400 pairs!
  (D) No mistakes

8.
  (F) I found out how to plant a
  (G) seed and make it grow. It
  (H) grew into a beautiful plant.
  (J) No mistakes

9.
  (A) Shandra shook her head.
  (B) She had missed the bus again,
  (C) and she knew shed be late for school.
  (D) No mistakes

10.
  (F) 308 Market Street
  (G) Farmland, MI 44567
  (H) May 14 2002
  (J) No mistakes

11.
  (A) Dear Sir,
  (B) I am returning this watch. It has not worked since I got it in the mail.
  (C) Please refund my money?
  (D) No mistakes

12.
  (F) I will expect a reply soon.
  (G) Sincerely
  (H) Albert Jones
  (J) No mistakes

For items 13–15, read each sentence with a blank. Choose the word or words that fit best in the blank and that show correct punctuation.

13. **Please wash your _____ car today.**
  (A) father's
  (B) Father's
  (C) fathers'
  (D) fathers's

14. **_____ don't forget your backpack.**
  (F) Tran
  (G) Tran:
  (H) Tran,
  (J) Tran;

15. **We will be going to _____ this summer.**
  (A) Washington: D.C.
  (B) Washington, dc
  (C) washington dc
  (D) Washington, D.C.,

STOP

LANGUAGE: LANGUAGE MECHANICS

● Lesson 2: Capitalization & Punctuation

Examples

For items A and 1–2, choose the sentence that shows correct punctuation and capitalization.

A.
- Ⓐ Rudy gave janet a gift.
- Ⓑ We can leave now but, the party isn't until seven.
- Ⓒ Do you think she will be surprised?
- Ⓓ This cake looks wonderful?

For items B and 3–13, choose the best way to write the underlined part. If the underlined part is correct, choose "Correct as is."

B. Winters are warm in <u>Tucson Arizona.</u>
- Ⓕ Tucson, arizona
- Ⓖ Tucson Arizona,
- Ⓗ Tucson, Arizona.
- Ⓙ Correct as is

 Remember to look for *correct* capitalization *and* punctuation.

● Practice

1.
- Ⓐ Suzie whispered, "This is a great movie."
- Ⓑ "Don't forget your money said Mother."
- Ⓒ Are there seats up front?" asked Bruce?
- Ⓓ "let's get popcorn" suggested Wanda.

2.
- Ⓕ Mrs. Shields writes about sports for our local newspaper.
- Ⓖ Did Dr. Robinson call yet.
- Ⓗ Please give this to miss Young.
- Ⓙ This is Mr McCoy's bicycle.

3. **Somehow, the shoe landed on <u>Felipe sanchez's lawn.</u>**
- Ⓐ felipe sanchez's lawn
- Ⓑ Felipe Sanchez's lawn
- Ⓒ Felipe Sanchez's Lawn
- Ⓓ Correct as is

4. **Rachel bought a new <u>necklace but somehow she lost it.</u>**
- Ⓕ necklace but,
- Ⓖ necklace, but
- Ⓗ necklace. But
- Ⓙ Correct as is

5. **"Don't change the <u>channel," yelled</u> Ben's little sister.**
- Ⓐ channel" yelled
- Ⓑ channel." Yelled
- Ⓒ channel." yelled
- Ⓓ Correct as is

GO ON

LANGUAGE: LANGUAGE MECHANICS

● Lesson 2: Capitalization & Punctuation (cont.)

Ricky said, "Watch **(6)** what I can do."
He rode his bike to the middle of the driveway.
And **(7)** balanced himself on the back wheel.
Il'I bet **(8)** there isn't another kid in mayfield
who **(9)** can do that.

6.
- (F) said, Watch
- (G) said, "watch
- (H) said "Watch
- (J) Correct as is

7.
- (A) driveway and
- (B) driveway and,
- (C) driveway And
- (D) Correct as is

8.
- (F) Ill bet
- (G) Ill' bet
- (H) I'll bet
- (J) Correct as is

9.
- (A) mayfield. Who
- (B) Mayfield who
- (C) mayfield, who
- (D) Correct as is

January 5 2001, **(10)**
dear Burt **(11)**
My mom said you are coming to see us next
month. If the weather is right, we can go
skiing, sledding, or **(12)** ice skating. You can
borrow my brother's skis and skates.
See you soon.
Your Cousin, **(13)**
Sarah

10.
- (F) January 5, 2001
- (G) January 5 2001
- (H) January 5, 2001,
- (J) Correct as is

11.
- (A) Dear Burt
- (B) dear burt
- (C) Dear Burt,
- (D) Correct as is

12.
- (F) skiing sledding or
- (G) skiing, sledding, or,
- (H) skiing sledding or,
- (J) Correct as is

13.
- (A) Your Cousin
- (B) Your cousin,
- (C) your Cousin,
- (D) Correct as is

GO ON

LANGUAGE: LANGUAGE MECHANICS

● Lesson 2: Capitalization & Punctuation (cont.)

For items 14–15, read each sentence with a blank. Choose the answer that fits best in the blank and shows correct capitalization and punctuation.

14. Do you think we should go swimming,

_____

- (F) Sam?
- (G) sam.
- (H) sam!
- (J) Sam.

15. The new mall will open on _____ .

- (A) may 1 2002
- (B) May 1, 2002
- (C) may 1, 2002
- (D) May, 1, 2002

Read the passage below. For items 16–19, choose the answer that shows the best way to write the underlined part.

(1) Can you imagine finding a bottle with a message inside—or perhaps one containing money? (2) bottles may travel thousands of miles in the ocean. (3) Not long ago a child in new york found a bottle that had been washed up on the beach. (4) Inside was 1,700! (5) After waiting a year, the youngster was allowed to keep the money.

16. In sentence 1, money? is best written —

- (F) money!
- (G) money.
- (H) Money?
- (J) As it is

17. In sentence 2, bottles is best written —

- (A) Bottles;
- (B) Bottles,
- (C) Bottles
- (D) As it is

18. In sentence 3, new york is best written —

- (F) New York
- (G) New York,
- (H) New york
- (J) As it is

19. In sentence 4, 1,700! is best written —

- (A) 1700.
- (B) $1,700!
- (C) $1,700?
- (D) As it is

STOP

LANGUAGE: LANGUAGE MECHANICS
SAMPLE TEST

● **Directions:** For items A and 1–4, choose the punctuation mark that is needed in the sentence. For items 5–6, choose the line that has a punctuation error. For items 7–8, choose the answer that fits best in the blank and shows correct punctuation.

Example

A. Its more fun than scary.

- Ⓐ ?
- Ⓑ !
- Ⓒ ,
- Ⓓ None

---

1. The puppy couldn't find the food dish.

- Ⓐ ,
- Ⓑ .
- Ⓒ ?
- Ⓓ None

2. Max said hed help me rake the leaves.

- Ⓕ "
- Ⓖ ,
- Ⓗ ?
- Ⓙ None

3. Why isnt he here?

- Ⓐ ?
- Ⓑ .
- Ⓒ ,
- Ⓓ None

4. Mom said, "Never sit on the arm of the couch."

- Ⓕ ,
- Ⓖ ?
- Ⓗ "
- Ⓙ None

5.

- Ⓐ "Don't forget to feed the
- Ⓑ hamster before you leave,
- Ⓒ Mom said.
- Ⓓ No mistakes

6.

- Ⓕ My violin competition was one of
- Ⓖ the best experiences Ive ever
- Ⓗ had. I felt very proud.
- Ⓙ No mistakes

7. Do you know what he got you for your
_____

- Ⓐ birthday?
- Ⓑ birthday.
- Ⓒ birthday!
- Ⓓ birthday:

8. _____ take a walk this afternoon," Jane suggested.

- Ⓕ Lets
- Ⓖ Lets'
- Ⓗ "Let's,
- Ⓙ "Let's

GO ON

Name _____   Date_____

For items 9–12, read each sentence. Choose the sentence that shows correct punctuation and capitalization.

9. Ⓐ my sister takes good notes.
    Ⓑ This is a good bird book
    Ⓒ What kind of bird was that?
    Ⓓ Did you put seed in the feeder.

10. Ⓕ The tennis courts are full
    Ⓖ Venus put our names on the list.
    Ⓗ Did you remember your racket.
    Ⓙ This can of tennis balls is new?

11. Ⓐ Dad bought seeds plants, and fertilizer.
    Ⓑ The shovel rake and hoe are in the garage.
    Ⓒ We usually camp with Jan, Bob and, Annie.
    Ⓓ The garden had corn, beans, and peas.

12. Ⓕ I cant see the game from here.
    Ⓖ Kim wasn't able to play this week.
    Ⓗ Don't' worry if you forgot.
    Ⓙ The coach would'nt let us in.

For items 13–16, read each sentence with a blank. Choose the answer that fits best in the blank and shows correct capitalization and punctuation.

13. **The neighbors got back from a long trip to the _____**
    Ⓐ south of china.
    Ⓑ south of China.
    Ⓒ South of china?
    Ⓓ South of China.

14. **_____ take the trash out now!" yelled Mom.**
    Ⓕ "Ahmed,
    Ⓖ Ahmed,
    Ⓗ "Ahmed
    Ⓙ "ahmed,

15. **Does that look like the _____**
    Ⓐ Grand Canyon.
    Ⓑ Grand Canyon?
    Ⓒ grand canyon?
    Ⓓ grand canyon.

16. **_____ he isn't going to join us.**
    Ⓕ No
    Ⓖ No:
    Ⓗ No;
    Ⓙ No,

GO ON

Name _____   Date_____

For items 17–20, read each sentence. Choose the sentence that shows correct punctuation and capitalization. If the underlined part is correct, choose "Correct as is."

17. The last thing I meant to do was annoy the Andersons on arbor day.

- (A) annoy the andersons on arbor day
- (B) Annoy The Andersons on arbor day
- (C) annoy the Andersons on Arbor Day
- (D) Correct as is

18. New zealand is home to a playful bird called the kea.

- (F) New, Zealand
- (G) new zealand
- (H) New Zealand
- (J) Correct as is

19. "Ouch! I've got a splinter in my finger," cried Rosa.

- (A) finger." Cried Rosa
- (B) finger," cried rosa
- (C) finger, cried Rosa
- (D) Correct as is

20. Potatoes are a healthful food but potato chips are not.

- (F) food. But potato
- (G) food, but potato
- (H) food; but potato
- (J) Correct as is

For items 21–24, read the passage. Choose the answer that shows the best way to write the underlined section. If the underlined section is correct, choose "Correct as is."

People who live in Nova Scotia Canada **(21)** are called Bluenoses. This isnt **(22)** because of the color of their noses, however. This part of Canada **(23)** once sold large quantities of potatoes called bluenose potatoes. The potatoes got their name because each one had a blue end or "nose. **(24)**

21.
- (A) Nova Scotia, Canada
- (B) Nova Scotia, Canada,
- (C) Nova Scotia, canada
- (D) Correct as is

22.
- (F) isnt'
- (G) is'nt
- (H) isn't
- (J) Correct as is

23.
- (A) Canada
- (B) Canada,
- (C) , Canada
- (D) Correct as is

24.
- (F) "nose.'
- (G) "nose".
- (H) "nose."
- (J) Correct as is

GO ON

Read the passage below. For items 25–28, choose the answer that shows the best way to write the underlined part.

(1) London Bridge" is often sung today as young children play a simple game. (2) The rhyme has many verses. (3) Some verses tell about things that did not happen? (4) But the first verse is different. (5) It tells about when the real london bridge of the 1100s was destroyed by attacking Norse warriors. (6) The other verses tell about efforts to build the bridge again.

25. **In sentence 1, London Bridge" is best written —**
    (A) "London Bridge"
    (B) London Bridge
    (C) "London bridge"
    (D) As it is

26. **In sentence 3, happen? is best written —**
    (F) Happen?
    (G) happen!
    (H) happen.
    (J) As it is

27. **In sentence 5, london bridge is best written —**
    (A) London bridge
    (B) London Bridge
    (C) London Bridge,
    (D) As it is

28. **In sentence 5, Norse is best written —**
    (F) norse
    (G) "norse"
    (H) "Norse"
    (J) As it is

STOP

Name _____ Date _____

LANGUAGE: LANGUAGE EXPRESSION

● **Lesson 3: Usage**

╭─────────── **Examples** ───────────╮

For items A and 1–3, read each sentence with a blank. Choose the word or phrase that fits best in the sentence.

A. **Pablo was looking _____ to his family's camping trip.**

- Ⓐ foremost
- Ⓑ forehead
- Ⓒ former
- Ⓓ forward

For items B and 4–6, read each sentence. Choose the answer that is a complete and correctly written sentence.

B.
- Ⓕ To take good notes.
- Ⓖ Some birds feed early.
- Ⓗ Using a computer.
- Ⓙ A detailed wall chart.

 Clue If you are not sure which answer is correct, eliminate answers you know are wrong and then take your best guess. Stay with your first answer choice. You should change an answer only if you are sure the one you marked is incorrect.

● **Practice**

1. **Carmina _____ left a chocolate bar on the camp table.**
   - Ⓐ angry
   - Ⓑ carelessly
   - Ⓒ bravely
   - Ⓓ have

2. **The water _____ in the fountain.**
   - Ⓕ splash
   - Ⓖ having splashed
   - Ⓗ splashing
   - Ⓙ splashed

3. **My mother _____ for three hours.**
   - Ⓐ drive
   - Ⓑ driven
   - Ⓒ has drove
   - Ⓓ drove

4.
   - Ⓕ Those muffins was delicious!
   - Ⓖ Those blueberries is so sweet and juicy.
   - Ⓗ We have picked them yesterday afternoon.
   - Ⓙ Please have another muffin.

5.
   - Ⓐ Sunday Simon did pitched for the Eagles.
   - Ⓑ Simon the Eagles on Sunday.
   - Ⓒ On Sunday, Simon pitched for the Eagles.
   - Ⓓ Pitched Simon did.

6.
   - Ⓕ I'd like an ham and cheese omelet?
   - Ⓖ Dan ate a sandwich and an apple.
   - Ⓗ Jake have a cup of soup and a salad.
   - Ⓙ May I please have a extra cookie?

 GO ON

Name _____ Date _____

LANGUAGE: LANGUAGE EXPRESSION

● **Lesson 3: Usage (cont.)**

For items 7–12, read each line. Choose the line that has a usage error. If there is no error, choose "No mistakes."

7.
  (A) George Washington
  (B) are called the father
  (C) of our country.
  (D) No mistakes

8.
  (F) Binoculars are helpful
  (G) because they let you
  (H) observe things closely.
  (J) No mistakes

9.
  (A) We missed the
  (B) baseball game however
  (C) there was a train crossing.
  (D) No mistakes

10.
  (F) The junior high
  (G) play take place on
  (H) Friday and Saturday night.
  (J) No mistakes

11.
  (A) He hasn't never made
  (B) a mistake on any of
  (C) his reading assignments.
  (D) No mistakes

12.
  (F) We haveta get more
  (G) decorations for the hall
  (H) in order to finish.
  (J) No mistakes

For items 13–14, read each sentence. Choose the answer that shows the best way to write the underlined part. If the underlined part is correct, choose "No changes."

13. Mr. Jacobs <u>leading</u> the school band.
  (A) leaded
  (B) leads
  (C) are leading
  (D) No changes

14. Pablo's family drove up the mountain on a long, <u>whiny</u> road.
  (F) wind
  (G) windshield
  (H) winding
  (J) No changes

For items 15–16, read each sentence. Choose the answer that is a complete and correctly written sentence.

15.
  (A) Ray and I raked the leaves into a huge pile.
  (B) My friend Ann helped him and I.
  (C) Her and I jumped onto the leaf pile
  (D) Ray's great picture of me and her.

16.
  (F) Not all birds.
  (G) Ostriches and penguins can't fly.
  (H) Fly in a V-shaped group.
  (J) Ducks and geese

GO ON

LANGUAGE: LANGUAGE EXPRESSION

● **Lesson 3: Usage (cont.)**

For items 17–20, read the paragraph and answer the questions.

(1) "Boy, does this sound like a goofy assignment," I said to Kendra, <u>rolling</u> my eyes. (2) We were walking home after school talking about what Mr. Stewart had given us for homework this week.

(3) We were supposed to listen—just listen—for two hours this week. (4) We could do it any time we wanted, in short periods or long, and write down some of <u>the stuffs</u> we heard. (5) We also had to describe where we listened and the time of day.

(6) As we walked by a park, Kendra stopped for a moment and suggested, "Hey, I have an idea. <u>Let's us</u> start right now."

(7) For once she had something. (8) I told her it was a great idea, then spotted <u>an bench</u> beside the fountain. (9) "Let's get started," I said.

17. In sentence 1, <u>rolling</u> is best written —

- Ⓐ rollering
- Ⓑ rolleded
- Ⓒ rolled
- Ⓓ As it is

18. In sentence 4, <u>the stuffs</u> is best written —

- Ⓕ the stuff
- Ⓖ a stuffs
- Ⓗ an stuff
- Ⓙ As it is

19. In sentence 6, <u>Let's us</u> is best written —

- Ⓐ Lets
- Ⓑ Lets us
- Ⓒ Let's
- Ⓓ As it is

20. In sentence 8, <u>an bench</u> is best written —

- Ⓕ an benches
- Ⓖ a bench
- Ⓗ a benches
- Ⓙ As it is

STOP

Name _____ Date_____

● **Lesson 4: Sentences**

Examples

For items A and 1–3, read each sentence. Choose the answer that names the simple subject.

A. It was mostly black with red marks on its
Ⓐ   Ⓑ   Ⓒ
wings.
Ⓓ

For items B and 4–6, read each sentence. Choose the answer that names the simple predicate.

B. Two people listen better than one
   Ⓕ   Ⓖ   Ⓗ   Ⓙ
person.

If you are not sure which answer is correct, say each one to yourself. The correct answer usually sounds best. Read the directions for each section and think about them when you choose the answer you think is correct.

● **Practice**

1. Everyone drinks orange juice for breakfast.
    Ⓐ   Ⓑ   Ⓒ Ⓓ

2. Most students enjoy camping.
   Ⓕ   Ⓖ   Ⓗ   Ⓙ

3. Charlotte lost her job because she showed up late.
   Ⓐ   Ⓑ Ⓒ   Ⓓ

4. It is important to eat a good breakfast.
  ⒻⒼ   Ⓗ   Ⓙ

5. I took Jake's dog Ben for a walk.
  Ⓐ   Ⓑ   Ⓒ   Ⓓ

6. Studying helps you get good grades.
   Ⓕ   Ⓖ   Ⓗ Ⓙ

GO ON

Name _____ Date _____

● **Lesson 4: Sentences (cont.)**

For items 7–8, read both sentences. Choose the answer that best combines the underlined sentences.

7. The traffic was loud.
    The neighbors were loud.
    I couldn't sleep.

    Ⓐ The traffic was loud and the neighbors were loud. I couldn't sleep.

    Ⓑ The traffic was loud. The neighbors were loud, but I couldn't sleep.

    Ⓒ The traffic and neighbors were loud, so I couldn't sleep.

    Ⓓ The traffic was loud and so were the neighbors; but I couldn't sleep.

8. Our town's name is Lost City.
    It has an unusual history.

    Ⓕ Lost City has an unusual history, and it is our town.

    Ⓖ An unusual history, our town is Lost City.

    Ⓗ Our town, Lost City, has an unusual history.

    Ⓙ With an unusual history, our town is Lost City.

For items 9–10, read each sentence. Choose the best way of expressing the idea.

9. Ⓐ The founders of Lost City from Baltimore came.

    Ⓑ The founders of Lost City came from Baltimore.

    Ⓒ Coming from Baltimore were the founders of Lost City.

    Ⓓ From Baltimore the founders of Lost City came.

10. Ⓕ Mary she rode the bus all the way into the city.

    Ⓖ Rode the bus all the way into the city Mary did.

    Ⓗ All the way into the city, Mary rode the bus.

    Ⓙ Mary rode the bus all the way into the city.

GO ON

LANGUAGE: LANGUAGE EXPRESSION

● Lesson 4: Sentences (cont.)

For items 11–14, read the passage and answer the questions.

(1) Serious storms are hurricanes that occur over the ocean. (2) The warm tropical ocean water is warm. (3) A low-pressure area forms above the waves, just as these areas often form during the summer and early fall. (4) The warm air zips up above the waves. (5) The moist air zips above the waves. (6) Cooler air in. (7) This causes the air to spin. (8) Air pressure in the center drops. (9) More warm, moist air is sucked up into the system. (10) It creates wind, rain, and clouds. (11) Inside the wall, the system's eye is calm. (12) But around the eye, the rain, wind, and clouds swirl in the fierce hurricane.

11. Sentence 1 is best written —

Ⓐ   Serious storms that occur over the ocean are hurricanes.

Ⓑ   Serious storms, hurricanes, occur over the ocean.

Ⓒ   Hurricanes are serious storms that occur over the ocean.

Ⓓ   As it is

12. Which sentence incorrectly repeats a word or group of words?

Ⓕ   Sentence 1

Ⓖ   Sentence 2

Ⓗ   Sentence 3

Ⓙ   Sentence 4

13. Which of these is not a sentence?

Ⓐ   Sentence 2

Ⓑ   Sentence 6

Ⓒ   Sentence 9

Ⓓ   Sentence 11

14. How can sentences 4 and 5 best be joined without changing their meanings?

Ⓕ   Zipping up above the waves, the water is warm and moist.

Ⓖ   The warm and moist air zips up above the waves.

Ⓗ   The warm air and the moist air zips up above the waves.

Ⓙ   The warm, moist air zips up above the waves.

LANGUAGE: LANGUAGE EXPRESSION

● Lesson 5: Paragraphs

Directions: Read the directions for each section. Choose the answer you think is correct.

Example

Read the paragraph. Choose the best topic sentence for the paragraph.

A. _____ . Most are in the highlands of the Southwest. The horses find great difficulty in getting food during the winter months. Snow covers the grass and small bushes that they feed on. Their numbers grow smaller each year.

- Ⓐ Horses have soft fur.
- Ⓑ Horses are interesting animals.
- Ⓒ There are about 20,000 wild horses living in our country.
- Ⓓ Horses can be ridden for work or for recreation.

 Clue Remember, a paragraph should focus on one idea. The correct answer is the one that fits best with the rest of the paragraph.

● Practice

Read the paragraph. Choose the best topic sentence for the paragraph.

1. _____ . Some said that if people dreamed of the same thing three nights in a row the dream was bound to come true. Others believed that if a person told about the dream before breakfast it would bring bad luck.

- Ⓐ People dream for lots of reasons.
- Ⓑ Long ago, people had many superstitions about dreams.
- Ⓒ Dreams can be about many different things.
- Ⓓ People used to be very superstitious.

Choose the answer that best develops the topic sentence below.

2. **Birds eat many different things.**

- Ⓕ Their colors vary from drab to colorful. Some drab birds have small patches of color.
- Ⓖ Small birds generally eat seeds and insects. Larger birds eat small animals and even fish.
- Ⓗ They also fly in different ways. Gulls soar, but hummingbirds flap their wings often.
- Ⓙ Even in cities, birds can survive. Some hawks now make their homes in skyscrapers.

 GO ON

LANGUAGE: LANGUAGE EXPRESSION

● Lesson 5: Paragraphs (cont.)

For items 3–4, read each paragraph. Choose the sentence that does not belong.

3. **(1)** The sleepy little fishing town doubled in size almost overnight. **(2)** Harriet Johnson decided to build a resort on the cliffs near the beach. **(3)** With her fortune, she hired hundreds of workers to complete the job. **(4)** Many of them decided to stay when the job was finished. **(5)** Mrs. Johnson lived to be 97 years old. **(6.)** These workers helped build the logging industry that exists even today.

    (A) Sentence 2
    (B) Sentence 3
    (C) Sentence 4
    (D) Sentence 5

4. **(1)** Loch Ness is a long and very deep lake in Scotland. **(2)** Since the year 565, many people there have told of seeing a strange animal with a long, snakelike neck and a small head. **(3)** Most of those who have seen it say the Loch Ness Monster is dark, has a hump like a camel, and is about 50 feet long. **(4)** Camels live in desert regions and can go long periods of time without drinking water.

    (F) Sentence 1
    (G) Sentence 2
    (H) Sentence 3
    (J) Sentence 4

For items 5–6, read each paragraph. Choose the sentence that fits best in the blank.

5. In Tennessee there is a large, beautiful lake inside a giant cave. _____ . Years ago people named it the "Lost Sea." In the 1800s, Native Americans and Southern soldiers would hide in the cave by the lake. This cave was once even used as a dance hall.

    (A) Tennessee also has beautiful mountains.
    (B) Lakes are usually filled with fresh water.
    (C) Caves can contain stalactites or stalagmites.
    (D) It is the world's largest underground lake.

6. You've heard of "raining cats and dogs," but how about fish? In an English town called Appin, thousands of herring fish fell from the sky one day in 1817. _____ . Today scientists think a storm sucked the fish up from the ocean and dumped them inland.

    (F) No one then could explain how this happened.
    (G) Fish are usually found in water.
    (H) Herring are a type of fish that people eat.
    (J) There weren't many modern conveniences in 1817.

GO ON

LANGUAGE: LANGUAGE EXPRESSION

● Lesson 5: Paragraphs (cont.)

For items 7–8, read the paragraph and answer the questions.

(1) One important reformer of the mid-1800s was Margaret Fuller. (2) As a young woman, Margaret Fuller taught school and wrote articles for magazines and newspapers. (3) She would hold public meetings with women to talk about issues that were important to them. (4) Women enjoy talking together about what interests them. (5) In 1845, Margaret Fuller also wrote a book on her ideas about women's rights. (6) Many people were excited about her ideas. (7) Sadly, Margaret Fuller died in 1850 on board a boat sailing for America.

7. Choose the best first sentence for this paragraph.

   (A) During the 1800s, many people introduced new inventions.

   (B) A reformer is someone who works to make conditions better than they have been.

   (C) Many important people lived during the 1800s.

   (D) Margaret is kind of an old-fashioned name.

8. Which sentence should be left out of this paragraph?

   (F) Sentence 3

   (G) Sentence 4

   (H) Sentence 1

   (J) Sentence 7

9. Which of the following would be most appropriate in a letter asking for information about sports programs available through a local community education program?

   (A) I have heard that you have a lot of neat programs for people in the community. I think this is a wonderful service you are providing that is much needed by those who can't afford to get such education anywhere else.

   (B) I am a very athletic person and am interested in what sports programs you will be offering during the summer. Please send me a schedule of programs that includes costs and times of meetings.

   (C) My family just moved here from Nebraska, and I am excited about meeting new people. I love to do active things.

   (D) I have volunteered in many places in the past and am wondering if you take volunteer instructors. Please send me a volunteer form.

GO ON

LANGUAGE: LANGUAGE EXPRESSION

● **Lesson 5: Paragraphs (cont.)**

For items 10–13, read the report and answer the questions.

(1) Thomas Jefferson accomplished many great things. (2) He is probably best known as the main author of the Declaration of Independence. (3) Jefferson was a person of integrity, and many people trusted him. (4) He was a member of the Continental Congress and a minister to France. (5) He became Secretary of State in 1790 and Vice President in 1797. (6) Jefferson served as President of the United States from 1801–1809. (7) His wife was not alive to be his first lady. (8) This great man continued to work for his principles until he passed away in 1826.

10. **Which of these could not be added after sentence 2?**

(F) Jefferson was tall, with reddish hair.

(G) He was only 33 years old when he helped write the Declaration.

(H) The Declaration of Independence was the first step in a war against Britain.

(J) Benjamin Franklin helped Jefferson with some of the ideas in the document.

11. **What is the topic sentence of the paragraph?**

(A) Sentence 1

(B) Sentence 2

(C) Sentence 3

(D) Sentence 4

12. **Which of these could be added after sentence 6?**

(F) He was president for seven years.

(G) During his presidency, he helped the United States purchase the Louisiana Territories.

(H) Some people liked him and some didn't.

(J) He was only the eighth President of the United States.

13. **Which sentence does not belong in the paragraph?**

(A) Sentence 5

(B) Sentence 6

(C) Sentence 7

(D) Sentence 8

STOP

LANGUAGE: LANGUAGE EXPRESSION
SAMPLE TEST

● **Directions:** Read the directions for each section. Choose the answer you think is correct.

Example

For item A, read the sentence. Choose the answer that names the simple predicate.

A.   Finally they arrived at the campground.
     Ⓐ   Ⓑ   Ⓒ   Ⓓ

For item 1, read the sentence. Choose the word or phrase that fits best in the sentence.

1.   The horn players _____ in the city finals.

    Ⓐ competes
    Ⓑ is competing
    Ⓒ compete
    Ⓓ competing

For item 2, read the sentence. Choose the answer that is a complete and correctly written sentence.

2.   Ⓕ I was late because the bus broke down.
    Ⓖ I was late even though the bus broked down.
    Ⓗ I was late the bus broke down.
    Ⓙ I was late because the bus is broke.

For items 3–5, read each line. Choose the line that has a usage error. If there is no error, choose "No mistakes."

3.   Ⓐ When I went to college,
    Ⓑ everyone was surprised when
    Ⓒ I choosed art as my major.
    Ⓓ No mistakes

4.   Ⓕ Although all snakes
    Ⓖ have teeths, very few
    Ⓗ of them have fangs.
    Ⓙ No mistakes

5.   Ⓐ Her cousin, Alyson,
    Ⓑ is the most politest person
    Ⓒ I have ever met.
    Ⓓ No mistakes

For item 6, read the sentence. Choose the answer that names the simple subject.

6.   All children like fruits better than
    Ⓕ   Ⓖ   Ⓗ Ⓙ
   vegetables.

For item 7, read the sentence. Choose the answer that names the simple predicate.

7.   Kendra said her homework assignment
    Ⓐ   Ⓑ
   would be a breeze.
    Ⓒ   Ⓓ

GO ON ➡

Name _____ Date _____

For items 8–10, choose the answer that best combines the underlined sentences.

8. **Susan walked three miles today.**
   Karen walked three miles today.

   (F) Susan walked three miles today, and so did Karen.

   (G) Three miles were walked today by both Susan and Karen.

   (H) Susan and Karen walked three miles today.

   (J) Susan walked three miles today; Karen did, too.

9. **Sondra painted the fence.**
   Sondra cleaned the yard.

   (A) Sondra painted the fence; she cleaned the yard.

   (B) Sondra painted the fence; then she cleaned the yard.

   (C) Sondra painted the fence, and Sondra cleaned the yard.

   (D) Sondra painted the fence and cleaned the yard.

10. **Sasha prepared lunch.**
    The lunch was hot.
    The lunch was delicious.

    (F) Sasha prepared lunch. The lunch was hot and delicious.

    (G) Sasha prepared a hot and delicious lunch.

    (H) Sasha prepared a lunch, which was hot and delicious.

    (J) Sasha prepared a lunch that was hot and also delicious.

For items 11–12, choose the best way of expressing the idea.

11. (A) Toward San Francisco a group of pioneers thought they were headed.

    (B) San Francisco, they thought the pioneers were headed.

    (C) A group of pioneers thought they were headed toward San Francisco.

    (D) A group of pioneers toward San Francisco were headed.

12. (F) Lost City was soon known for its fine seafood.

    (G) Soon, Lost City was known for its fine seafood.

    (H) For its fine seafood, Lost City was known soon.

    (J) Lost City, for its fine seafood, was soon known.

GO ON

Read the paragraph. Choose the best topic sentence for the paragraph.

13. _____ . Soap was once money to the people of Mexico. Lumps of coal were used as coins by the people of England. Stone money was used on the Pacific Ocean island of Yep. Even food has been used as money. In Russia, "coins" of cheese could be used to buy things.

- (A) Soap can be made from animal fat.
- (B) Soap is often used to wash children's mouths out.
- (C) Money was not always made of metals or paper, as it is today.
- (D) Money has been around for a long time.

Choose the answer that best develops the topic sentence below.

14. **During colonial days there were no bathtubs or showers in houses.**

- (F) Colonial days were during the time that European people first settled in America.
- (G) There weren't any cars either. People had to travel by horse.
- (H) People today take lots of baths. In fact, some people even have swimming pools and hot tubs in their houses.
- (J) They were not missed, however. People of that time thought that baths were unhealthy.

Read the paragraph. Choose the sentence that does not belong.

15. **(1)** Rain is the biggest danger to baby birds. **(2)** During rainy weather, the parents have to leave the nest in search of food. **(3)** Baby birds usually eat chewed-up worms and bugs. **(4)** The baby birds are left uncovered. **(5)** The babies get chilled. **(6)** Thousands have been known to die during long rainstorms.

- (A) Sentence 1
- (B) Sentence 3
- (C) Sentence 4
- (D) Sentence 6

Read the paragraph. Choose the sentence that fits best in the blank.

16. **Today's cows produce much more milk than cows of the past. _____. Fifteen years ago, the average cow produced just 6,000 quarts of milk. In ancient times, cows produced only enough to feed their calves.**

- (F) Today, cows are much healthier.
- (G) Milk has many vitamins that growing children need.
- (H) Thanks to science, a modern cow produces 10,000 quarts of milk a year.
- (J) Farmers use modern milking machines.

GO ON

LANGUAGE: LANGUAGE EXPRESSION
SAMPLE TEST (cont.)

For items 17–20, read the passage and answer the questions.

(1) People in the city of Rabaul live in a huge volcanic crater. (2) Because of this, they know they need an escape plan in case of an eruption.

(3) In the fall of 1994, people began to notice signs of an eruption. (4) Recognized the signs. (5) Birds flew away from their nests; the ground shook in an up-and-down motion rather than side-to-side; and sea snakes slithered out of the ocean.

(6) On the day of the eruption, earthquakes shook Rabaul. (7) More than 50,000 people left the area. (8) Volcanic ash filled the sky.

(9) When the smoke cleared, about three-fourths of the houses on the island been flattened. (10) The island suffered greatly, but because of planning only a few people lost their lives.

17. How is sentence 2 best written?

- (A) They know they need an escape plan, because of this, in case of an eruption.
- (B) They know, because of this, that they need an escape plan in case of an eruption.
- (C) An escape plan in case of eruption because of this they need.
- (D) As it is

18. Which sentence could be added after sentence 5?

- (F) Animals can sense an earthquake long before people can feel the tremors.
- (G) Sea snakes are snakes that live in water.
- (H) The snakes slithered in a side-to-side motion.
- (J) The ocean nearby is filled with many creatures.

19. Which is not a complete sentence?

- (A) Sentence 1
- (B) Sentence 2
- (C) Sentence 3
- (D) Sentence 4

20. In sentence 9, been is best written —

- (F) have been
- (G) beened
- (H) had been
- (J) As it is

STOP

LANGUAGE: SPELLING

● **Lesson 6: Spelling**

Directions: For items A and 1–4, choose the word that is spelled correctly and fits best in the blank. For items B and 5–7, read each phrase. Choose the phrase in which the underlined word is not spelled correctly.

Examples

A. My teacher _____ that I practice my violin for one hour each day.

- (A) recommended
- (B) reccommended
- (C) reccomended
- (D) recomended

B.
- (F) daring rescue
- (G) solid rock
- (H) oister shell
- (J) blue plastic

 **Clue** Read the directions carefully. Be sure you know whether you need to look for the correctly spelled word or the incorrectly spelled word.

● **Practice**

1. Tomorrow will be _____ .
   - (A) rainee
   - (B) rainie
   - (C) ranie
   - (D) rainy

2. We went on a _____ walk.
   - (F) nachur
   - (G) nature
   - (H) nayture
   - (J) nachure

3. The garage needed a _____ cleaning.
   - (A) thoroh
   - (B) thurow
   - (C) thourough
   - (D) thorough

4. Jonas is going to a _____ movie.
   - (F) horor
   - (G) horror
   - (H) horrorr
   - (J) horrer

5.
   - (A) avoid capture
   - (B) hate to complane
   - (C) empty room
   - (D) fourteen points

6.
   - (F) sparkle brightly
   - (G) confusing siginal
   - (H) shallow water
   - (J) find something

7.
   - (A) receeved a call
   - (B) furious crowd
   - (C) cable channel
   - (D) white chalk

 GO ON

● Lesson 6: Spelling Skills (cont.)

Read each answer. Choose the answer that has a spelling error. If none have an error, choose "No mistakes."

8.
- (F) carnevore
- (G) citrus
- (H) fascinate
- (J) No mistakes

9.
- (A) conceited
- (B) invention
- (C) ceese
- (D) No mistakes

10.
- (F) cricket
- (G) consider
- (H) asignment
- (J) No mistakes

Read each phrase. Choose the underlined word that is misspelled for how it is used in the phrase.

11.
- (A) reed a book
- (B) grew up
- (C) mountain summit
- (D) tipped over

12.
- (F) bad attitude
- (G) high sees
- (H) butter and bread
- (J) incorrect answer

13.
- (A) active child
- (B) taking notes
- (C) supporting sentences
- (D) buzzing be

Read each sentence. Choose the underlined part that is misspelled. If all words are spelled correctly, choose "No mistake."

14. Some plants eat meat in adition to eating
    (F)   (G)
    their own food. No mistake
    (H)   (J)

15. Usually the bones of birds' wings are
    (A)   (B)
    hollow. No mistake
    (C)   (D)

16. One bauld eagle nest can weigh as
    (F)   (G)
    much as an automobile. No mistake
    (H)   (J)

17. It is said that one milun matches can be
    (A)   (B)   (C)
    made from one tree. No mistake
    (D)

STOP

Name _____   Date _____

LANGUAGE: SPELLING
SAMPLE TEST

For items A and 1–4, choose the word that is spelled correctly and fits best in the blank.

A.   We need a new _____ _____ .

   (A) vidio recorder
   (B) video recorder
   (C) video recordor
   (D) vidio ricorder

For items B and 5–9, read each phrase. Choose the phrase in which the underlined word is *not* spelled correctly.

B.   (F) aired desert
   (G) pumpkin pie
   (H) will disappoint
   (J) giggle loudly

1.   This _____ leads to the gym.

   (A) stareway
   (B) stareweigh
   (C) stairweigh
   (D) stairway

2.   Three _____ people lived in the city.

   (F) milion
   (G) millun
   (H) millione
   (J) million

3.   Did you finish the _____ yet?

   (A) lesson
   (B) leson
   (C) lessin
   (D) lessan

4.   We planted _____ along the fence.

   (F) daisyes
   (G) daisies
   (H) daisys
   (J) daises

5.   (A) traffic sounds
   (B) five minutes
   (C) amazing student
   (D) loud grone

6.   (F) draw concloosions
   (G) curious cat
   (H) disappointing day
   (J) make comparisons

7.   (A) excited kids
   (B) venomous snakes
   (C) dog hare
   (D) detect sound

8.   (F) pioneer town
   (G) save mony
   (H) fine seafood
   (J) rescue boat

9.   (A) mountain gorila
   (B) crisp lettuce
   (C) porcupine quills
   (D) large building

GO ON

LANGUAGE: SPELLING
SAMPLE TEST (cont.)

Read each answer. Choose the answer that has a spelling error. If none have an error, choose "No mistakes."

10.
- (F) reproduce
- (G) usualy
- (H) interest
- (J) No mistakes

11.
- (A) service
- (B) fountain
- (C) suceed
- (D) No mistakes

12.
- (F) cautius
- (G) observe
- (H) information
- (J) No mistakes

Read each phrase. Choose the underlined word that is misspelled for how it is used in the phrase.

13.
- (A) groan up
- (B) second chance
- (C) spelling bee
- (D) wrap carefully

14.
- (F) terrible food
- (G) famous legend
- (H) dew your homework
- (J) amusing play

15.
- (A) airborne sounds
- (B) human population
- (C) beautiful flower
- (D) roll play

Read each sentence. Choose the underlined part that is misspelled. If all words are spelled correctly, choose "No mistake."

16. Alaskan huskies need five thowsand
(F)
calories and up to four quarts of water a
(G)   (H)
day. No mistake
(J)

17. During the winter in Japan, they make
(A)
elaborate stachues out of ice and snow.
(B)   (C)
No mistake
(D)

18. The five-pound kiwi bird can lay an egg
(F)
weighing more than a pound! No mistake
(G)   (H)   (J)

19. Harriet Tubman asited slaves in escaping
(A)   (B)
by using the Underground Railroad.
(C)
No mistake
(D)

STOP

Name _____ Date _____

LANGUAGE: STUDY SKILLS

● Lesson 7: Study Skills

Directions: Read the directions for each section. Choose the answer you think is correct.

Example

Table of Contents	
Chapter	**Page**
1 Kinds of Bugs 1	
2 Bug Bodies 15	
3 Bug Senses 29	
4 What Bugs Eat 37	

A. Which chapter probably tells about how bugs find food?

- Ⓐ Chapter 1
- Ⓑ Chapter 2
- Ⓒ Chapter 3
- Ⓓ Chapter 4

 Clue Look at all the answer choices before you mark the one you think is correct. Be sure the answer circle you fill in is the same letter as the answer you think is correct.

● Practice

Use the picture of encyclopedias to do items 1–2.

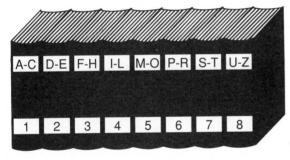

1. In which volume would you find information about different types of flags?

- Ⓐ Volume 2
- Ⓑ Volume 3
- Ⓒ Volume 5
- Ⓓ Volume 7

2. Which of the following topics would be found in Volume 5?

- Ⓕ information about the moon
- Ⓖ how to knit
- Ⓗ world climate regions
- Ⓙ the life of Marian Anderson

3. Look at these guidewords from a dictionary page.

> fourth–fragile

Which of the following could be found on this page?

- Ⓐ frail
- Ⓑ fourteenth
- Ⓒ fracture
- Ⓓ fountain

4. Look at these guidewords from a dictionary page.

> pace–packing

Which of the following could be found on this page?

- Ⓕ package
- Ⓖ pac
- Ⓗ pact
- Ⓙ pad

GO ON

Name _____ Date_____

● **Lesson 7: Study Skills (cont.)**

Based on the graph below, choose the best answer for items 5–8.

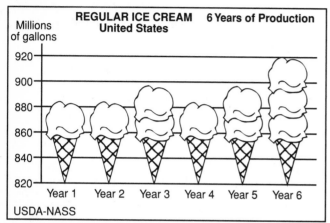

REGULAR ICE CREAM   6 Years of Production
United States
Millions of gallons
USDA-NASS

5. Which year showed the highest ice cream production?

- (A) Year 3
- (B) Year 4
- (C) Year 5
- (D) Year 6

6. Approximately how many millions of gallons of ice cream were produced in Year 3?

- (F) 897 million gallons
- (G) 900 million gallons
- (H) 880 million gallons
- (J) 890 million gallons

7. Which year deviates from a pattern of increasing production?

- (A) Year 1
- (B) Year 2
- (C) Year 3
- (D) Year 4

8. Based on the graph, which of the following statements is true?

- (F) Ice cream production decreased overall from Year 1 to Year 6.
- (G) Ice cream production increased at a steady rate.
- (H) Ice cream production increased overall from Year 1 to Year 6.
- (J) One hundred million more gallons of ice cream were produced in Year 6 than Year 1.

STOP

Name _____   Date _____

LANGUAGE: STUDY SKILLS
SAMPLE TEST

● **Directions:** Read the directions for each section. Choose the answer you think is correct.

Examples

A. In which resource would you look to find the population density of New York City?

- (A) dictionary
- (B) newspaper
- (C) card catalog
- (D) atlas

B. What is the name of the part of a book in which references are listed?

- (F) bibliography
- (G) table of contents
- (H) index
- (J) glossary

Use the sample dictionary entries below to answer the questions.

crush (krŭsh) v. 1. To press between opposing bodies; to break or hurt. 2. To subdue. 3. To overwhelm. n. 1. A large crowd. 2. A usu. short-lived foolish attraction. 3. The object of a short-lived foolish attraction. 4. A critical moment.

crusty (krŭs'tē) adj. 1. Having, being, or being like a crust. 2. Coarse or rough in manner.

crutch (krŭch) n. 1. A support made to help with walking usu. held under the arm and sometimes used in pairs. 2. The leg rest on a sidesaddle. 3. A device used as a support or prop. v. 1. To support or prop up.

1. The *u* in *crush* sounds most like the vowel sound in the word —

- (A) urge
- (B) us
- (C) took
- (D) horrid

2. Which definition best fits the word *crush* as it is used in the sentence below?

There was a huge crush as the concert hall doors opened.

- (F) n. 1.
- (G) n. 4.
- (H) n. 3.
- (J) n. 2.

3. Which is the correct way to divide *crusty* into syllables?

- (A) c-rus-ty
- (B) cr-us-ty
- (C) cr-us-t-y
- (D) crus-ty

4. In which of these sentences is *crutch* used as a verb?

- (F) David had to use a crutch after he sprained his foot.
- (G) He crutched up the table with a tall stick.
- (H) Lee used his baby blanket as a crutch to make him braver.
- (J) Ravi threw her leg around the crutch as she sat in the saddle.

Raina and Miguel have decided to open their own pizza shop. Answer the following questions to help them plan.

5. **Where should they look to find out how many competitors they will have in the area?**

   Ⓐ encyclopedia under *business*
   Ⓑ dictionary under *pizza*
   Ⓒ Yellow Pages of the phone book
   Ⓓ atlas

6. **Where could they go to find out about different pizza recipes?**

   Ⓕ library
   Ⓖ city hall
   Ⓗ fire station
   Ⓙ county court

7. **Raina and Miguel will use this web while they interview workers. What other word best fits in the blank oval?**

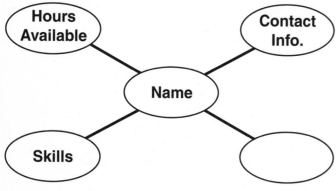

   Ⓐ Pizza Preference
   Ⓑ Experience
   Ⓒ Family Members
   Ⓓ Sales Receipts

Study the table of contents from a book titled *Sunken Treasures*. Read each question and choose the correct answer.

Table of Contents	
Chapter	Page
1 Types of Treasures	1
2 Places Treasures Have Been Found	14
3 People Who Have Studied Treasures	28
4 How Treasure Ships Sank	46
5 Sunken Treasures Not Yet Found	62
6 Web Site References About Sunken Treasure	75
7 Book References About Sunken Treasure	83
8 Periodical References About Sunken Treasure	92

8. **Yoshi wants to do more investigating about sunken treasure. In which chapters should she look?**

   Ⓕ Chapters 1, 2, and 3
   Ⓖ Chapters 3, 4, and 5
   Ⓗ Chapters 4, 5, and 6
   Ⓙ Chapters 6, 7, and 8

9. **Which of the following sentences might be found in Chapter 1?**

   Ⓐ The Caribbean is a place many people think of when they hear the words *sunken treasure*.
   Ⓑ One valuable site is *www.yo-ho-matey.com*.
   Ⓒ Treasure ranges from ancient oil lamps to gold and jewels.
   Ⓓ Many treasure ships sank during fierce battles.

GO ON

Study this entry from an electronic card catalog to answer items 10–13.

AUTHOR: Lyons, Nick
TITLE: Confessions of a fly-fishing
      addict/Nick Lyons.
PUBLISHER: New York : Simon & Schuster,
      c1989
DESCRIPT: 200 p. : 22 cm
SUBJECTS: Fly fishing
ADD TITLE: Confessions of a fly-fishing addict
ISBN: 067168379
DYNIX #: 392312

Copy Details
LIBRARY: KDL-East Grand Rapids Branch
STATUS: on shelf
CALL NUMBER: 799.12 Lyo : 9/89

10. In what year was this book published?
- (F) 2000
- (G) 1989
- (H) 1799
- (J) None of these

11. Choose the label for the shelf on which you would look for this book.
- (A) 500–600
- (B) 600–700
- (C) 700–800
- (D) 800–900

12. What does the *Lyo* in the call number stand for?
- (F) the month it was purchased
- (G) the title
- (H) the library branch
- (J) the author's last name

13. In which section of the library might you go to find more books about fly-fishing?
- (A) 500s
- (B) 600s
- (C) 700s
- (D) 800s

Study the outline and then do items 14–15.

Owls
  I. _____
      A. Great Horned Owl
      B. Snowy Owl
      C. Barn Owl
  II. Body Characteristics
      A. Size
      B. Body Covering
      C. _____
      D. Eyes, Talons, and Beaks
  III. Eating Habits
      A. Mice
      B. Other Small Rodents

14. Which of the following fits best in the blank next to I.?
- (F) Owl Status
- (G) Owl Habitats
- (H) Types of Owls
- (J) Owl Reproduction

15. Which of the following fits best in the blank next to C.?
- (A) Feather Variations
- (B) Grasses and Leaves
- (C) Trees
- (D) Nocturnal

STOP

ANSWER SHEET

STUDENT'S NAME

| LAST | FIRST | MI |

SCHOOL

TEACHER

FEMALE ◯   MALE ◯

BIRTH DATE

| MONTH | DAY | YEAR |

JAN ◯ FEB ◯ MAR ◯ APR ◯ MAY ◯ JUN ◯ JUL ◯ AUG ◯ SEP ◯ OCT ◯ NOV ◯ DEC ◯

GRADE

③ ④ ⑤

Part 1: LANGUAGE MECHANICS

A	Ⓐ Ⓑ Ⓒ Ⓓ
1	Ⓐ Ⓑ Ⓒ Ⓓ
2	Ⓕ Ⓖ Ⓗ Ⓙ
3	Ⓐ Ⓑ Ⓒ Ⓓ
4	Ⓕ Ⓖ Ⓗ Ⓙ
5	Ⓐ Ⓑ Ⓒ Ⓓ
6	Ⓕ Ⓖ Ⓗ Ⓙ
7	Ⓐ Ⓑ Ⓒ Ⓓ
8	Ⓕ Ⓖ Ⓗ Ⓙ
9	Ⓐ Ⓑ Ⓒ Ⓓ
10	Ⓕ Ⓖ Ⓗ Ⓙ
11	Ⓐ Ⓑ Ⓒ Ⓓ
12	Ⓕ Ⓖ Ⓗ Ⓙ
13	Ⓐ Ⓑ Ⓒ Ⓓ
14	Ⓕ Ⓖ Ⓗ Ⓙ
15	Ⓐ Ⓑ Ⓒ Ⓓ
16	Ⓕ Ⓖ Ⓗ Ⓙ
17	Ⓐ Ⓑ Ⓒ Ⓓ
18	Ⓕ Ⓖ Ⓗ Ⓙ
19	Ⓐ Ⓑ Ⓒ Ⓓ
20	Ⓕ Ⓖ Ⓗ Ⓙ

Part 2: LANGUAGE EXPRESSION

A	Ⓐ Ⓑ Ⓒ Ⓓ
1	Ⓐ Ⓑ Ⓒ Ⓓ
2	Ⓕ Ⓖ Ⓗ Ⓙ
3	Ⓐ Ⓑ Ⓒ Ⓓ
4	Ⓕ Ⓖ Ⓗ Ⓙ
5	Ⓐ Ⓑ Ⓒ Ⓓ
6	Ⓕ Ⓖ Ⓗ Ⓙ
7	Ⓐ Ⓑ Ⓒ Ⓓ
8	Ⓕ Ⓖ Ⓗ Ⓙ
9	Ⓐ Ⓑ Ⓒ Ⓓ
10	Ⓕ Ⓖ Ⓗ Ⓙ
11	Ⓐ Ⓑ Ⓒ Ⓓ
12	Ⓕ Ⓖ Ⓗ Ⓙ
13	Ⓐ Ⓑ Ⓒ Ⓓ
14	Ⓕ Ⓖ Ⓗ Ⓙ
15	Ⓐ Ⓑ Ⓒ Ⓓ
16	Ⓕ Ⓖ Ⓗ Ⓙ
17	Ⓐ Ⓑ Ⓒ Ⓓ
18	Ⓕ Ⓖ Ⓗ Ⓙ
19	Ⓐ Ⓑ Ⓒ Ⓓ
20	Ⓕ Ⓖ Ⓗ Ⓙ

Part 3: SPELLING

A	Ⓐ Ⓑ Ⓒ Ⓓ
B	Ⓕ Ⓖ Ⓗ Ⓙ
1	Ⓐ Ⓑ Ⓒ Ⓓ
2	Ⓕ Ⓖ Ⓗ Ⓙ
3	Ⓐ Ⓑ Ⓒ Ⓓ
4	Ⓕ Ⓖ Ⓗ Ⓙ
5	Ⓐ Ⓑ Ⓒ Ⓓ
6	Ⓕ Ⓖ Ⓗ Ⓙ
7	Ⓐ Ⓑ Ⓒ Ⓓ
8	Ⓕ Ⓖ Ⓗ Ⓙ
9	Ⓐ Ⓑ Ⓒ Ⓓ
10	Ⓕ Ⓖ Ⓗ Ⓙ
11	Ⓐ Ⓑ Ⓒ Ⓓ
12	Ⓕ Ⓖ Ⓗ Ⓙ
13	Ⓐ Ⓑ Ⓒ Ⓓ
14	Ⓕ Ⓖ Ⓗ Ⓙ
15	Ⓐ Ⓑ Ⓒ Ⓓ
16	Ⓕ Ⓖ Ⓗ Ⓙ
17	Ⓐ Ⓑ Ⓒ Ⓓ
18	Ⓕ Ⓖ Ⓗ Ⓙ
19	Ⓐ Ⓑ Ⓒ Ⓓ

Part 4: STUDY SKILLS

A	Ⓐ Ⓑ Ⓒ Ⓓ
1	Ⓐ Ⓑ Ⓒ Ⓓ
2	Ⓕ Ⓖ Ⓗ Ⓙ
3	Ⓐ Ⓑ Ⓒ Ⓓ
4	Ⓕ Ⓖ Ⓗ Ⓙ
5	Ⓐ Ⓑ Ⓒ Ⓓ
6	Ⓕ Ⓖ Ⓗ Ⓙ
7	Ⓐ Ⓑ Ⓒ Ⓓ
8	Ⓕ Ⓖ Ⓗ Ⓙ
9	Ⓐ Ⓑ Ⓒ Ⓓ
10	Ⓕ Ⓖ Ⓗ Ⓙ
11	Ⓐ Ⓑ Ⓒ Ⓓ
12	Ⓕ Ⓖ Ⓗ Ⓙ
13	Ⓐ Ⓑ Ⓒ Ⓓ
14	Ⓕ Ⓖ Ⓗ Ⓙ

LANGUAGE PRACTICE TEST

● Part 1: Language Mechanics

Directions: Read each sentence. Choose the punctuation mark that is needed in the sentence. If no more punctuation is needed, choose "None."

Example

A.   **Look out, here comes an avalanche**

   - (A) **!**
   - (B) **.**
   - (C) **?**
   - (D) None

1.   **I ate the whole box I had such a stomachache.**
   - (A) **,**
   - (B) **!**
   - (C) **;**
   - (D) None

2.   **Oranges lemons, and grapefruits are citrus fruits.**
   - (F) **?**
   - (G) **,**
   - (H) **;**
   - (J) None

3.   **"That closet needs a thorough cleaning! my mom said.**
   - (A) **"**
   - (B) **.**
   - (C) **'**
   - (D) None

4.   **We've been waiting anxiously.**
   - (F) **.**
   - (G) **'**
   - (H) **?**
   - (J) None

For items 5–6, choose the line that has a punctuation error. If there is no error, choose "No mistakes."

5.
   - (A) The bus will pick us up
   - (B) at 830 a.m. sharp for
   - (C) the field trip to the zoo.
   - (D) No mistakes

6.
   - (F) Sara wanted to adopt
   - (G) another greyhound but
   - (H) she simply didn't have room.
   - (J) No mistakes

For items 7–8, choose the word or words that fit best in the blank and show correct punctuation.

7.   **_____ we won't be seeing that film.**
   - (A) No
   - (B) No,
   - (C) No;
   - (D) No:

8.   **_____ and Russ all went to get their hair cut.**
   - (F) Max Mikey
   - (G) Max, Mikey,
   - (H) Max Mikey,
   - (J) Max Mikey;

GO ON

For items 9–12, read each sentence. Choose the sentence that shows correct punctuation and capitalization.

9. (A) Tell Mrs Jensen I called.
    (B) Miss. Richards will be late.
    (C) Our coach is Mr. Wannamaker
    (D) Dr. Cullinane was here earlier.

10. (F) Will you please take the garbage out.
    (G) Dont let Rachel forget her chores.
    (H) She has been reading *Charlotte's Web* all afternoon.
    (J) This house looks like a pigsty

11. (A) "I suggest you go the library to do research," Mom said.
    (B) "The *world book* encyclopedia is a good place to look."
    (C) "I will help you look in *National Geographic* when you get home."
    (D) Your report will be perfect when your done," Mom insisted.

12. (F) Joel hurt his wrist, yesterday while playing hockey.
    (G) However, he scored three goals in the process.
    (H) He will be the champion of patterson Ice Center.
    (J) Perhaps they will loan him the stanley cup

For items 13–16, read each sentence with a blank. Choose the answer that fits best in the blank and shows correct capitalization and punctuation.

13. **The play will be held on Wednesday, _____ nights.**
    (A) Thursday, and Friday,
    (B) Thursday, and, Friday
    (C) Thursday, and Friday
    (D) Thursday and Friday,

14. **_____ for the cool camera.**
    (F) Thank you,
    (G) thank you
    (H) Thank, you
    (J) Thank you

15. **Our project is due on _____ .**
    (A) october 28 2002
    (B) October 28, 2002
    (C) October 28 2002
    (D) October, 28, 2002

16. **Please send that to _____ .**
    (F) Mankato, Minnesota
    (G) mankato Minnesota
    (H) mankato minnesota
    (J) mankato, Minnesota,

GO ON

LANGUAGE PRACTICE TEST

Part 1: Language Mechanics (cont.)

For items 17–20, read the passage. Choose the correct answer for each question.

Dear grandma

(1) Guess where we went today? (2) We went to see the Statue of Liberty. (3) I couldn't believe how big it is. (4) Theres a huge torch in the statue's hand. (5) I could see the statue as we sailed across to it. (6) It looked big from the boat, but it was gigantic when I stood in front of it.

(7) Yesterday we took the elevator up to the top of the Empire State Building. (8) We used telescopes to look out across the city. (9) We were up so high!

(10) Dad says it's time to go. (11) We're going to Central Park today to skate row on the lake, and feed ducks. (12) I'm going to mail your letter in the hotel lobby. (13) See you soon?

Love,

Delia

17. At the beginning of Delia's letter, Dear grandma is best written —

- (A) Dear Grandma
- (B) Dear Grandma,
- (C) Dear Grandma.
- (D) As it is

18. In sentence 4, Theres is best written —

- (F) There's
- (G) Theres'
- (H) Theres's
- (J) As it is

19. In sentence 10, skate row on the lake, and feed ducks. is best written —

- (A) skate row on the lake and feed ducks,
- (B) skate row on the lake and feed ducks.
- (C) skate, row on the lake, and feed ducks.
- (D) As it is

20. In sentence 13, See you soon? is best written —

- (F) See you Soon.
- (G) See you soon
- (H) See you soon.
- (J) As it is

STOP

LANGUAGE PRACTICE TEST

● Part 2: Language Expression

Directions: Read the directions for each section. Choose the answer you think is correct.

Example

For item A, read the sentence. Choose the answer that names the simple subject.

A.   We need to learn to type faster so we can get our work done on time.
   Ⓐ Ⓑ   Ⓒ   Ⓓ

For item 1, choose the word or phrase that fits best in the sentence.

1.   The ball _____ down the steps.

   Ⓐ   rolled
   Ⓑ   roll
   Ⓒ   rolling
   Ⓓ   having rolled

For item 2, choose the answer that is a complete and correctly written sentence.

2.   Ⓕ   Last night at 7 o'clock in the school auditorium.

   Ⓖ   The third annual school talent show.

   Ⓗ   Our class put on the funniest skit of the show.

   Ⓙ   Heard my parents laughing and applauding.

For items 3–5, read each line. Choose the line that has a usage error. If there is no error, choose "No mistakes."

3.   Ⓐ   Me and Paige want to
   Ⓑ   go horseback riding this
   Ⓒ   Saturday if the weather is good.
   Ⓓ   No mistakes

4.   Ⓕ   It wasn't no bother to
   Ⓖ   retype that paper since
   Ⓗ   I had to do mine too.
   Ⓙ   No mistakes

5.   Ⓐ   Please clean up the dinner
   Ⓑ   dishes before you start
   Ⓒ   watching television.
   Ⓓ   No mistakes

For item 6, read the sentence. Choose the answer that names the simple subject.

6.   The show must go on if we want to win
   Ⓕ Ⓖ   Ⓗ
   the state theater competition.
                     Ⓙ

For item 7, read the sentence. Choose the answer that names the simple predicate.

7.   Please turn in papers that include your
   Ⓐ   Ⓑ   Ⓒ   Ⓓ
   name and the date.

GO ON

LANGUAGE PRACTICE TEST
Part 2: Language Expression (cont.)

For items 8–10, read both sentences. Choose the answer that best combines the underlined sentences.

8. **The tiny squirrel peeked from behind the tree.**
    The tiny squirrel scurried away.

    F The tiny squirrel peeked and scurried away from behind the tree.

    G The tiny squirrel peeked from behind the tree; it scurried away.

    H The tiny squirrel peeked from behind the tree and scurried away.

    J The tiny squirrel peeked from behind the tree and the tiny squirrel scurried away.

9. **Maxine arrived at 6 o'clock.**
    Sylvia arrived at 6 o'clock.

    A Maxine arrived at 6 o'clock; so did Sylvia.

    B Maxine arrived at 6 o'clock and Sylvia arrived at 6 o'clock.

    C Maxine arrived at 6 o'clock, as did Sylvia.

    D Maxine and Sylvia arrived at 6 o'clock.

10. **Janie has a bicycle.**
    Her bike is shiny.
    Her bike is green.

    F Janie has a bicycle. It is shiny and green.

    G Janie has a shiny, green bicycle.

    H Janie has a shiny bicycle. Janie has a green bicycle.

    J Janie has a bicycle, which is shiny and green.

For items 11–12, read each sentence. Choose the best way of expressing the idea.

11. A Having burned dead wood and heavy brush.

    B They burn dead wood and heavy brush.

    C Dead wood and heavy brush they burn.

    D Dead wood will burn heavy brush.

12. F The workers in the logging industry that exists today helped build.

    G These workers, they helped build the logging industry. It exists even today.

    H These workers helped build the logging industry that exists even today.

    J These workers the logging industry that exists even today helped build.

Name _____ Date_____

Read the paragraph. Choose the best topic sentence for the paragraph.

13. _____ . One scientist found out that cars painted pink or any light shade seem to be safer. The light colors are more easily seen. Cars of two or three different colors may be even safer.

    (A) Cars can come in many colors

    (B) If prefer my cars to be red.

    (C) Scientists counted car accidents to look for ways to prevent them.

    (D) Scientists study natural phenomenon.

Choose the answer that best develops the topic sentence below.

14. **The Gulf Stream is made up of a flow of warm ocean water a thousand times as great as the flow of the Amazon River.**

    (F) Scientists have mapped the Gulf Stream's course up the Atlantic Coast.

    (G) Hot springs also have warm water.

    (H) The Amazon River is in South America.

    (J) Water also flows down rivers and streams toward the oceans.

Read the paragraph. Choose the sentence that does not belong.

15. **(1)** Niagara Falls, one of the world's biggest waterfalls, is partly in the United States and partly in Canada. **(2)** My family went there for our vacation last summer. **(3)** In 1969, scientists did a strange thing at the falls. **(4)** They shut off the American falls for several months by building a big dam across the river so no water could get to the falls. **(5)** The scientists wanted to study the rocks underneath the water.

    (A) Sentence 1

    (B) Sentence 2

    (C) Sentence 4

    (D) Sentence 5

Read the paragraph. Choose the sentence that fits best in the blank.

16. **One of the nicest things about summer evenings is being able to watch fireflies or try to catch them. _____ . Some scientists think the lights are used to scare away birds that might eat the fireflies. Others think the fireflies use their lights to say "hello" to their future mates.**

    (F) My grandma likes to sit on the porch in the evening.

    (G) I usually catch fireflies in a big jam jar.

    (H) Fireflies need to have lots of air if you catch them and put them in a jar.

    (J) Did you ever wonder why fireflies light up?

GO ON

LANGUAGE PRACTICE TEST

Part 2: Language Expression (cont.)

For items 17–20, read the passage. Choose the best answer for each question.

(1) There are more than 15,000 active volcanoes in the world. **(2)** Still, know everything there is to know about volcanoes scientists do not. **(3)** The study of volcanoes is called volcanology, and people who study volcanoes are called volcanologists.

(4) How does a volcano form? **(5)** Hot liquid rock, called magma, bubbles toward the surface through rock. **(6)** Once magma has arrived at the earth's surface, it is called lava. **(7)** Lava builds up until it forms a mountain in the shape of a cone. **(8)** The spot where lava comes up to the earth's surface through the cone is called a volcano.

(9) Some volcanic eruptions calm, but others destructive. **(10)** Large pieces of rock can be thrown out of the volcano. **(11)** People near an erupting volcano can be in great danger from <u>flowing</u> lava and volcanic bombs.

17. Sentence 2 is best written —

- Ⓐ Scientists still don't know everything there is to know about volcanoes.
- Ⓑ Scientists don't know everything there is to know about volcanoes still.
- Ⓒ Scientists don't still know everything there is to know about volcanoes.
- Ⓓ As it is

18. Which of these is not a sentence?

- Ⓕ Sentence 8
- Ⓖ Sentence 9
- Ⓗ Sentence 10
- Ⓙ Sentence 11

19. Which sentence could be added after Sentence 10?

- Ⓐ Some people collect these rocks after the eruption.
- Ⓑ Dust is also thrown out and can cloud the air.
- Ⓒ Rocks are also formed from flowing lava.
- Ⓓ Many people like to bring back rock souvenirs when they visit a volcano.

20. In Sentence 11, <u>flowing</u> is best written —

- Ⓕ flowdering
- Ⓖ flowering
- Ⓗ flowed
- Ⓙ As it is

STOP

Name _____ Date_____

● **Part 3: Spelling**

Directions: Read the directions for each section. Choose the answer you think is correct.

Examples

For items A and 1–4, choose the word that is spelled correctly and fits best in the blank.

A. **Alexa sure was _____ about visiting her grandma!**
- (A) exited
- (B) excited
- (C) exsited
- (D) ecsited

For items B and 5–9, read each phrase. Choose the phrase in which the underlined word is not spelled correctly for how it is used.

B.
- (F) college dormitory
- (G) assemble a toy
- (H) loyal dog
- (J) paws briefly

---

1. **The train _____ arrived.**
- (A) finaly
- (B) finnaly
- (C) finely
- (D) finally

2. **Please _____ your work.**
- (F) revew
- (G) reeview
- (H) review
- (J) revyoo

3. **He is my best _____ .**
- (A) frind
- (B) frend
- (C) friend
- (D) freind

4. **Please _____ your papers in number order.**
- (F) arange
- (G) arainge
- (H) arrainge
- (J) arrange

5.
- (A) hardest job
- (B) blond hare
- (C) good citizen
- (D) invite them

6.
- (F) no trouble
- (G) unusual bird
- (H) local seen
- (J) lively conversation

7.
- (A) stormy knight
- (B) ordered food
- (C) funny story
- (D) pineapple cake

8.
- (F) train passenger
- (G) threatened species
- (H) numerous ants
- (J) time two go

9.
- (A) spring day
- (B) ruff road
- (C) Tuesday morning
- (D) bird migration

GO ON

LANGUAGE PRACTICE TEST
Part 3: Spelling (cont.)

For items 10–12, read each answer. Choose the answer that has a spelling error. If none have an error, choose "No mistakes."

10. (F) broil
     (G) acident
     (H) dwarf
     (J) No mistakes

11. (A) jury
     (B) knuckle
     (C) pollite
     (D) No mistakes

12. (F) wildernes
     (G) structure
     (H) republic
     (J) No mistakes

For items 13–15, read each phrase. Choose the underlined word that is misspelled for how it is used in the phrase.

13. (A) ad numbers
     (B) brilliant diamond
     (C) distant planet
     (D) nibble cheese

14. (F) compound word
     (G) baron wasteland
     (H) science laboratory
     (J) publish a book

15. (A) blood vessel
     (B) olive oil
     (C) length of chord
     (D) mosquito net

For items 16–19, read each sentence. Choose the underlined part that is misspelled. If all words are spelled correctly, choose "No mistake."

16. We should probly go inside before the
                (F)   (G)
     thunderstorm starts. No mistake
         (H)   (J)

17. Our dog always houls at the moon on
                  (A)   (B)
     Thursday nights. No mistake
         (C)   (D)

18. The weather forecast for this weekend
              (F)   (G)
     looks postitive. No mistake
          (H)   (J)

19. Sharon was completing a puzzle with her
                    (A)   (B)
     classmate Marty. No mistake
         (C)   (D)

STOP

Name _____ Date_____

LANGUAGE PRACTICE TEST

● Part 4: Study Skills

Directions: Study the schedule. Then choose the correct answer to the question.

Example

SCHEDULE

9:00	Clean Room
10:00	Take out Trash
10:30	Walk Dog
11:00	Clean Bathroom
11:30	Clean Kitchen
12:00	Lunch
12:30	Water Houseplants
1:00	Water Garden
1:30	Go to Grocery Store

A. Study the schedule. What should you be doing at 11:30?

- (A) Eating lunch
- (B) Taking out the trash
- (C) Cleaning the kitchen
- (D) Walking the dog

Study the map. Read items 1–4 and choose the correct answer.

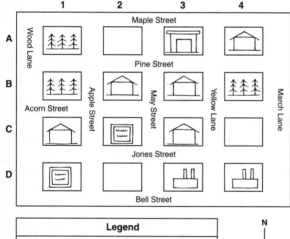

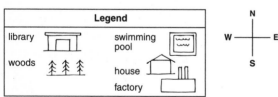

1. Near which coordinate is the library located?

- (A) B-2
- (B) A-3
- (C) D-3
- (D) C-1

2. Where are the factories located?

- (F) west of Apple Street
- (G) on the north side of the city
- (H) on the south side of the city
- (J) south of Bell Street

3. How many wooded areas does this town have?

- (A) 1
- (B) 2
- (C) 3
- (D) 4

4. If you walked from the library toward one of the swimming pools, you would be going —

- (F) southeast
- (G) northwest
- (H) northeast
- (J) southwest

LANGUAGE PRACTICE TEST
Part 4: Study Skills (cont.)

For items 5–9, choose the best answer for each question.

5. **Where would you look to find the phone number for a plumber?**
   - (A) encyclopedia
   - (B) newspaper
   - (C) telephone book
   - (D) atlas

6. **Which resource would you use to find out when Hanukkah occurs this year?**
   - (F) encyclopedia
   - (G) calendar
   - (H) dictionary
   - (J) atlas

7. **Where would you look to find a word that means the same as another word?**
   - (A) dictionary
   - (B) crossword puzzle
   - (C) encyclopedia
   - (D) thesaurus

8. **Which would you find in the glossary of a book?**
   - (F) the year the book was published
   - (G) the meanings of words from the book
   - (H) the titles of the book chapters
   - (J) the topics found in the book and where to find them

9. **Which of the following would probably appear on a map of your state?**
   - (A) locations of gas stations
   - (B) lakes, rivers, and major waterways
   - (C) the street where you live
   - (D) the location of your city hall

For items 10–13, choose the word or name that would come first if the list was arranged in alphabetical order.

10.
   - (F) door
   - (G) dog
   - (H) double
   - (J) dragon

11.
   - (A) annoy
   - (B) hoot
   - (C) horn
   - (D) ancient

12.
   - (F) Joling, Beth
   - (G) Omar, Elijah
   - (H) Appleton, John
   - (J) Harkness, Dan

13.
   - (A) Davis, Pam
   - (B) Davis, Renee
   - (C) Davis, Rob
   - (D) Davis, Sasha

Read the sentences. Choose the answer that shows key words that should be included in notes on Frederick Douglass.

14. **Frederick Douglass was probably born in 1818. He became a well-known author, speaker, and reformer on the subject of the abolition of slavery.**
   - (F) Frederick Douglass; well-known speaker; slavery
   - (G) Frederick Douglass; born 1818; reformer; abolition of slavery
   - (H) 1818; author; speaker; abolition
   - (J) probably;1818; author; abolition

MATH: CONCEPTS

● Lesson 1: Numeration

Directions: Read and work each problem. Choose the correct answer and mark it.

Examples

A. Which of the following is an odd number and a multiple of 3?

- (A) 6
- (B) 9
- (C) 24
- (D) 11

B. The following is a list of how many baseball cards these friends collected: Tanya—207, Mercedes—287, Jared—278, and Lance—239. Which of the following answers shows the baseball card collections arranged from least cards to most?

- (F) Tanya, Lance, Mercedes, Jared
- (G) Tanya, Lance, Jared, Mercedes
- (H) Lance, Tanya, Mercedes, Jared
- (J) Mercedes, Jared, Lance, Tanya

 Clue Look at all the answer choices before you choose. Make sure you fill in the answer circle completely.

● Practice

1. Yusef is in line to take his turn at the long jump. There are 13 people in line, and he is in the middle. What is his place in line?

- (A) fifth
- (B) tenth
- (C) seventh
- (D) sixth

2. There are an even number of events in which students can participate at the May Day fair. Which of the following could be the number of events?

- (F) 11
- (G) 15
- (H) 21
- (J) 22

3. What is 547 rounded to the nearest hundred?

- (A) 550
- (B) 560
- (C) 500
- (D) 600

4. Colleen found 16 shells on Saturday and 17 shells on Sunday. Al found 12 shells on Saturday and 22 shells on Sunday. Who found the greater number of shells altogether?

- (F) Al
- (G) Colleen
- (H) They found the same number of shells.
- (J) Not enough information

GO ON

Name _____ Date _____

MATH: CONCEPTS

● **Lesson 1: Numeration (cont.)**

5. **What number goes in the box on the number line shown?**

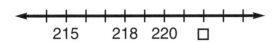

215   218 220 ☐

   (A) 230
   (B) 224
   (C) 222
   (D) 228

6. **Which number is between 456,789 and 562,325?**

   (F) 572,325
   (G) 564,331
   (H) 455,644
   (J) 458,319

7. **If these numbers are put in order from greatest to least, what is the number exactly in the middle?**

45 55 50 65 30 35 75

   (A) 45
   (B) 50
   (C) 35
   (D) 30

8. **Look at the numbers below. If these numbers are ordered from least to greatest, which answer choice would correctly fit?**

33,616 255,500 4,580,000 _____

   (F) 887,140,000
   (G) 88,846
   (H) 3,540,939
   (J) 2,193

9. **What is $15.67 rounded to the nearest dollar?**

   (A) $15.00
   (B) $15.50
   (C) $16.00
   (D) $15.60

10. **Choose the most reasonable answer. What is the average number of books in a bookstore?**

   (F) 100
   (G) 1,000,000
   (H) 10,000
   (J) 600

11. **Which group of numbers is in order from least to greatest?**

   (A) 4, 34, 16, 66, 79
   (B) 13, 24, 35, 44, 65
   (C) 76, 89, 45, 13, 12
   (D) 3, 56, 12, 98, 10

12. **Which of these numbers is even and a multiple of 12?**

   (F) 35
   (G) 145
   (H) 144
   (J) 148

13. **Which of the following will have a remainder when divided by 6?**

   (A) 12
   (B) 42
   (C) 36
   (D) 46

STOP

MATH: CONCEPTS

● Lesson 2: Number Concepts

Directions: Read and work each problem. Choose the correct answer and mark it.

Examples

A. Which number has an 8 in the thousands place?

- Ⓐ 81,428
- Ⓑ 78,643
- Ⓒ 42,638
- Ⓓ 29,821

B. What is the meaning of 1,976?

- Ⓕ one thousand nine hundred seventy-six
- Ⓖ one hundred ninety-six
- Ⓗ nineteen thousand seventy-six
- Ⓙ nineteen seventy-sixes

 Clue Look for key words in each problem. If you are stuck, skip the problem and come back to it at the end of this lesson.

● Practice

1. Two thousand fifty-six can be shown as —

- Ⓐ 20,056
- Ⓑ 256
- Ⓒ 2.56
- Ⓓ 2,056

2. What is 365 rounded to the nearest ten?

- Ⓕ 400
- Ⓖ 360
- Ⓗ 370
- Ⓙ 300

3. What does the 4 in 42,678 mean?

- Ⓐ 4,000
- Ⓑ 400
- Ⓒ 40,000
- Ⓓ 4

4. What is the next number in this sequence?

2 4 6 8 10 12 ...

- Ⓕ 16
- Ⓖ 14
- Ⓗ 20
- Ⓙ 13

5. What number can be expressed as the following?

(8 x 2) + 4

- Ⓐ 10
- Ⓑ 14
- Ⓒ 20
- Ⓓ 23

6. 768 =

- Ⓕ seven sixty-eight
- Ⓖ seventeen hundred sixty-eight
- Ⓗ seven hundred sixty-eight
- Ⓙ seven thousand sixty-eight

GO ON

MATH: CONCEPTS

● Lesson 2: Number Concepts (cont.)

7. What is the meaning of 690?

   (A) 69 hundreds

   (B) 6 hundreds and 9 ones

   (C) 69 tens

   (D) 6 hundreds and 9 tens

8. Which number can be expressed as $(14 + 5) + (9 \times 3) - 1$?

   (F) 30

   (G) 31

   (H) 46

   (J) 45

9. What is the correctly written expanded numeral for 265?

   (A) 200 + 60 + 5

   (B) 260 + 5

   (C) 2 + 6 + 5

   (D) 200 + 65

10. What is 42 in written form?

    (F) fourteen two

    (G) four two

    (H) forty-two

    (J) fourty-two

11. What is another way to write ten thousands?

    (A) 10 + 1,000

    (B) 1,000

    (C) ten 1,000

    (D) 10,000

12. Shawn is collecting stones for a project. On the first day, he collects 100. On the second day, he collects 20. On the third, he finds 3 stones. Which number shows how many stones he collected in all?

    (F) 23

    (G) 123

    (H) 1,023

    (J) 24

13. What is the standard form of 5,000 + 70 + 9?

    (A) 579,000

    (B) 5,790

    (C) 5,079

    (D) 579

14. What is the standard form of forty-two thousand nine hundred and one?

    (F) 42,910

    (G) 42,901

    (H) 4,291

    (J) 429,100

STOP

MATH: CONCEPTS

● **Lesson 3: Properties**

Directions: Read and work each problem. Choose the correct answer and mark it.

Examples

A. The sum of two numbers is 21 and their product is 98. What are the 2 numbers?

- (A) 12 and 8
- (B) 14 and 7
- (C) 77 and 21
- (D) 7 and 9

B. What number goes in the box to make this number sentence true?

- (F) 4
- (G) 1
- (H) 2
- (J) 3

$$\frac{\square}{4} = \frac{1}{2}$$

Clue

Read each problem carefully and be sure you understand what it is asking for. Double-check the letter of your answer choice before filling in the circle.

● **Practice**

1. Which number comes next in this pattern?

   5, 15, 45, _____

   - (A) 50
   - (B) 60
   - (C) 135
   - (D) None of these

3. What is 788 rounded to the nearest hundred?

   - (A) 700
   - (B) 780
   - (C) 790
   - (D) 800

2. The only charge to use the pool is the $3.00 parking fee. Which of these number sentences should be used to find how much money the parking lot made on a day when 82 cars were parked there?

   - (F) 82 + $3.00 =
   - (G) 82 − $3.00 =
   - (H) 82 x $3.00 =
   - (J) 82 ÷ $3.00 =

4. What equation would you use to find out the number of minutes in one week?

   - (F) 24 x 60
   - (G) (7 x 24) x 60
   - (H) (7 x 24) x 365
   - (J) 365 ÷ 60

GO ON

MATH: CONCEPTS

● **Lesson 3: Properties (cont.)**

5. There are two numbers whose product is 98 and quotient is 2. What are the two numbers?

   (A) 49 and 8
   (B) 14 and 2
   (C) 14 and 7
   (D) 96 and 2

6. Look at the problem below. Which of these symbols goes in the box to get the smallest answer?

   150 □ 6 =

   (F) +
   (G) −
   (H) x
   (J) ÷

7. What letter is missing from this pattern?

   CDE_____GCDEFG

   (A) C
   (B) A
   (C) G
   (D) F

8. Which number sentence goes with 5 + 32 = 37?

   (F) 37 − 32 = 5
   (G) 37 + 5 = 42
   (H) 32 x 5 = 160
   (J) 32 ÷ 8 = 4

9. The □ stands for what number?

   5 x □ = 200

   (A) 100
   (B) 40
   (C) 4
   (D) 25

10. Which equation will have the greatest answer?

    (F) 357 − 6 =
    (G) 615 − 485 =
    (H) 888 − 777 =
    (J) 915 − 769 =

11. Each column in the number pattern below equals 21. What numbers are missing?

3	5	2	1	6
2	7	8	9	1
9	8	4	6	7
__	1	7	__	7

    (A) 6 and 8
    (B) 7 and 5
    (C) 1 and 7
    (D) 4 and 3

12. Suppose you are estimating by rounding to the nearest ten. What numbers should you use to estimate if you are rounding numbers between 23 and 46?

    (F) 30 and 50
    (G) 30 and 40
    (H) 20 and 50
    (J) 20 and 40

STOP

Name _____   Date_____

● Lesson 4: Fractions & Decimals

Directions: Read and work each problem. Show each fraction in simplest form. Choose the correct answer and mark it.

Examples

A. $\frac{1}{4}$ is equal to which of the following?

- (A) 0.04
- (B) 0.40
- (C) 0.25
- (D) 0.50

B. Which number could be put in the empty box to make this statement true?

$\frac{8}{7} > \square$

- (F) $\frac{7}{8}$
- (G) 7
- (H) 8
- (J) 8.7

Clue Pay close attention to the numbers in the denominator and the placement of the decimal points. If you misread, you may choose the wrong answer.

● Practice

1. Which of these figures is $\frac{4}{7}$ shaded?

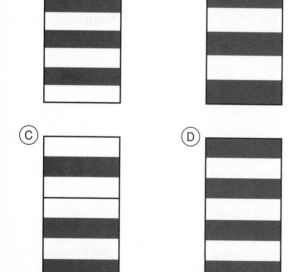

3. Marianne traveled 99.5 miles in one weekend. If she traveled 46.9 miles on Saturday, how far did she travel on Sunday?

- (A) 52.6 miles
- (B) 146.4 miles
- (C) 34 miles
- (D) Not enough information

2. What point represents $\frac{3}{4}$?

- (F) A
- (G) B
- (H) C
- (J) D

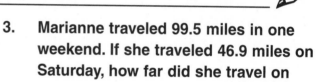

4. Which mixed number below is the same as $\frac{82}{9}$?

- (F) $1\frac{9}{9}$
- (G) $1\frac{1}{9}$
- (H) $9\frac{1}{9}$
- (J) 9

GO ON

● **Lesson 4: Fractions & Decimals (cont.)**

5. Which of the following numbers has a 5 in the hundredths place?

(A) 505.21
(B) 251.32
(C) 31.335
(D) 63.251

6. What picture shows a fraction equivalent to $\frac{3}{10}$?

(F)   (G)

(H)    (J)

7. Which of these has a value greater than $\frac{1}{8}$?

(A) $\frac{1}{16}$
(B) $\frac{9}{4}$
(C) $\frac{1}{32}$
(D) $\frac{1}{64}$

8. Which number shows how much of the figure below is shaded?

(F) $\frac{1}{2}$
(G) $\frac{2}{10}$
(H) $\frac{5}{1}$
(J) $\frac{5}{100}$

9. Which fraction shows how many of the shapes are shaded?

(A) $\frac{1}{3}$
(B) $\frac{2}{3}$
(C) $\frac{12}{4}$
(D) 3

10. Which of the decimals below names the smallest number?

(F) 2.15
(G) 2.05
(H) 2.50
(J) 2.21

11. Which fraction and decimal set below shows equal amounts?

(A) $\frac{1}{8}$ and 0.125
(B) $\frac{3}{4}$ and 0.34
(C) $\frac{1}{2}$ and 0.25
(D) $\frac{2}{10}$ and 0.02

12. How would 4.75 be represented as a fraction in simplest terms?

(F) $4\frac{3}{4}$
(G) $4\frac{7}{5}$
(H) $4\frac{3}{5}$
(J) $4\frac{75}{100}$

STOP

Name _____ Date _____

MATH: CONCEPTS
SAMPLE TEST

● **Directions:** Read and work each problem. Show each fraction in simplest form. Choose the correct answer and mark it.

Examples

A. Which of these is the best estimate of
$767 \div 7 = \square$?

- (A) 10
- (B) 11
- (C) 100
- (D) 110

B. Which symbol below best completes the equation?

$84.62 \ \square \ 84.26$

- (F) >
- (G) =
- (H) <
- (J) None of these

---

1. In this pyramid, each number is the product of the two numbers directly below it. Which number is missing from the pyramid?

48

8   ?

4   2   3

- (A) 6
- (B) 4
- (C) 8
- (D) None of these

2. How many hundreds are in 100,000?

- (F) 10
- (G) 100,000
- (H) 100
- (J) 1,000

3. Which of the following fraction groups are ordered correctly from least to greatest?

- (A) $1\frac{1}{8}, \ \frac{7}{8}, \ \frac{5}{8}, \ \frac{8}{8}$
- (B) $\frac{2}{3}, \ \frac{2}{5}, \ \frac{2}{4}, \ \frac{5}{6}$
- (C) $\frac{1}{2}, \ \frac{1}{3}, \ \frac{1}{4}, \ \frac{1}{6}$
- (D) $\frac{2}{10}, \ \frac{2}{8}, \ \frac{2}{5}, \ \frac{2}{3}$

4. What is 10,962 in written form?

- (F) nineteen thousand sixty-two
- (G) ten thousand nine hundred sixty-two
- (H) one thousand nine hundred sixty-two
- (J) ten thousand nine six two

GO ON

1-57768-974-7 *Spectrum Test Practice 4*

5. Which of the following is *not* a multiple of 3 that is less than 30?

   (A) 15
   (B) 6
   (C) 18
   (D) 19

6. Which number correctly completes the following related number sentences?

   $6 - 2 = \square$
   $2 + \square = 6$
   $6 - \square = 2$
   $\square + 2 = 6$

   (F) 4
   (G) 2
   (H) 3
   (J) 6

7. Which fraction names the greatest number?

   (A) $\frac{3}{4}$
   (B) $\frac{2}{3}$
   (C) $\frac{7}{8}$
   (D) $\frac{1}{2}$

8. What is 500,003,300 in correctly written expanded form?

   (F) 500,000,000 + 3,000 + 3
   (G) 500,000,000 + 30,000 + 30
   (H) 500,000 + 3,300
   (J) 500,000,000 + 3,000 + 300

9. What equation would you use to solve the following problem?

   Tyrone and Lawrence have a total of 26 CDs. They each have the same number of CDs. How many CDs does Tyrone have?

   (A) $26 \times 2 = \square$
   (B) $26 + 2 = \square$
   (C) $26 - 2 = \square$
   (D) $26 \div 2 = \square$

10. What fraction goes in the box on the number line below?

    (F) $\frac{3}{4}$
    (G) $\frac{1}{2}$
    (H) $\frac{2}{4}$
    (J) None of these

    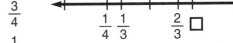

11. If you made 20 cookies and had to fit them into 4 boxes to give to your friends, how would you find the number of cookies to fit in each box?

    (A) add 20 and 4
    (B) subtract 4 from 20
    (C) multiply 20 by 4
    (D) divide 20 by 4

12. What is $73.52 rounded to the nearest dollar?

    (F) $73.50
    (G) $74.00
    (H) $73.00
    (J) $75.00

STOP

MATH: COMPUTATION

● Lesson 5: Addition & Subtraction of Whole Numbers

Directions: Choose the correct answer to each equation. Choose "None of these" if the correct answer is not given.

Examples

A.
```
  31
+ 25
```
- (A) 6
- (B) 56
- (C) 54
- (D) None of these

B.
```
 925
-   6
```
- (F) 919
- (G) 931
- (H) 4650
- (J) None of these

 Clue Pay special attention to the operation sign. Make sure you know whether to add or subtract.

● Practice

1.
```
  282
  422
+ 116
```
- (A) 810
- (B) 830
- (C) 710
- (D) None of these

2.
```
  995
- 226
```
- (F) 967
- (G) 1221
- (H) 769
- (J) None of these

3. $281 - 93 =$
- (A) 212
- (B) 374
- (C) 188
- (D) None of these

4.
```
  5,989
+ 2,697
```
- (F) 8,686
- (G) 8,668
- (H) 3,292
- (J) None of these

5.
```
  45
- 22
```
- (A) 23
- (B) 67
- (C) 990
- (D) None of these

6.
```
  76
- 23
```
- (F) 99
- (G) 53
- (H) 3
- (J) None of these

7. $96 + 52 + 48 =$
- (A) 196
- (B) 4
- (C) 148
- (D) None of these

8. $7 + \square = 71$
- (F) 10
- (G) 78
- (H) 64
- (J) None of these

STOP

Name _____ Date _____

MATH: COMPUTATION

● Lesson 6: Addition & Subtraction of Fractions

Directions: Choose the correct answer to each equation in simplest form. Choose "None of these" if the correct answer is not given.

Examples

A. $\frac{4}{5} + \frac{4}{5} =$

- (A) $\frac{5}{8}$
- (B) $1\frac{3}{5}$
- (C) 1
- (D) None of these

B. $1\frac{4}{7}$
$- \frac{3}{7}$

- (F) 2
- (G) $1\frac{1}{7}$
- (H) $\frac{17}{7}$
- (J) None of these

 Clue Look closely at the operation sign. Add whole numbers together first, then fractions. Remember to reduce to simplest form.

● Practice

1. $2\frac{1}{5}$
$+ 1\frac{3}{5}$

- (A) 4
- (B) $3\frac{4}{5}$
- (C) $3\frac{2}{5}$
- (D) None of these

2. $\frac{3}{4} - \frac{1}{4} =$

- (F) $\frac{4}{4}$
- (G) 1
- (H) $\frac{1}{2}$
- (J) None of these

3. $\frac{1}{10} + \frac{5}{10} = \square$

- (A) $\frac{10}{6}$
- (B) $\frac{3}{5}$
- (C) $\frac{6}{10}$
- (D) None of these

4. $\frac{5}{8} + \frac{7}{8} + \frac{1}{8} =$

- (F) $\frac{13}{8}$
- (G) $\frac{13}{24}$
- (H) $1\frac{5}{8}$
- (J) None of these

5. $\frac{6}{6} - \frac{6}{6} =$

- (A) 0
- (B) $\frac{12}{6}$
- (C) $\frac{0}{6}$
- (D) None of these

6. $\square - \frac{2}{9} = \frac{5}{9}$

- (F) $1\frac{1}{9}$
- (G) $\frac{3}{9}$
- (H) $\frac{7}{9}$
- (J) None of these

7. $\frac{7}{9}$
$- \frac{6}{9}$

- (A) $1\frac{4}{9}$
- (B) $\frac{13}{9}$
- (C) $\frac{1}{9}$
- (D) None of these GO ON

Name _____   Date_____

● **Lesson 6: Addition & Subtraction of Fractions (cont.)**

Choose the correct answer to each
equation in simplest form. Choose "None
of these" if the correct answer is not given.

8. $\frac{5}{6}$

    $+\frac{\square}{}$
    _____
    $1\frac{2}{3}$

    (F) $\frac{5}{6}$

    (G) 1

    (H) $\frac{7}{6}$

    (J) None of these

9. $\square - \frac{2}{3} = 0$

    (A) $\frac{2}{3}$

    (B) $1\frac{2}{3}$

    (C) 0

    (D) None of these

10. $1\frac{3}{14}$

     $-\frac{1}{14}$
     _____

     (F) $1\frac{2}{7}$

     (G) $1\frac{1}{7}$

     (H) $\frac{1}{7}$

     (J) None of these

11. $\frac{11}{12} - \frac{9}{12} =$

     (A) $\frac{1}{6}$

     (B) $\frac{2}{12}$

     (C) $1\frac{1}{2}$

     (D) None of these

12. $1\frac{7}{9}$

     $+\frac{5}{9}$
     _____

     (F) $2\frac{3}{9}$

     (G) $1\frac{12}{9}$

     (H) $2\frac{1}{3}$

     (J) None of these

13. $\frac{2}{3} - \square = \frac{1}{3}$

     (A) $\frac{3}{3}$

     (B) $\frac{1}{3}$

     (C) 1

     (D) None of these

14. $\frac{1}{24} + \frac{5}{24} =$

     (F) $\frac{1}{4}$

     (G) $\frac{4}{24}$

     (H) $\frac{6}{24}$

     (J) None of these

15. $\frac{3}{11} + \frac{9}{11} + \frac{1}{11} =$

     (A) $\frac{13}{11}$

     (B) $1\frac{2}{11}$

     (C) $\frac{5}{11}$

     (D) None of these

16. $\frac{2}{4} + \square = 1$

     (F) $\frac{1}{4}$

     (G) $\frac{2}{4}$

     (H) $1\frac{1}{2}$

     (J) None of these

STOP

MATH: COMPUTATION

● Lesson 7: Addition & Subtraction of Decimals

Directions: Choose the correct answer to each equation. Choose "None of these" if the correct answer is not given.

Examples

A. 6.211
    + 9.938

- (A) 16.149
- (B) 161.49
- (C) 160.149
- (D) None of these

B. 6.89 – 3.00 =

- (F) 9.89
- (G) 3.89
- (H) 6.92
- (J) None of these

 Clue The answer in an addition problem is always larger than the numbers being added.

● Practice

1. 0.6 – 0.6 =

- (A) 0
- (B) 0.12
- (C) 1
- (D) None of these

5. 1.5 + 2.9 =

- (A) 1.4
- (B) 4.4
- (C) 1.109
- (D) None of these

2. $0.57
    + 0.68

- (F) 1.25
- (G) $1.25
- (H) .125
- (J) None of these

6. $3.07 – $1.85 =

- (F) 122
- (G) $4.92
- (H) $1.22
- (J) None of these

3. 0.6537
    – 0.4325

- (A) 1.0862
- (B) 0.2212
- (C) 0.22
- (D) None of these

7. $24.59
    19.57
    + 28.36

- (A) $72.32
- (B) 72.52
- (C) $72.52
- (D) None of these

4. □ – 5.07 = 10.01

- (F) 15.08
- (G) 5.07
- (H) 4.94
- (J) None of these

8. 12.053 + □ = 17.002

- (F) 15.059
- (G) 29.055
- (H) 4.949
- (J) None of these

 STOP

Name _____   Date _____

MATH: COMPUTATION

● Lesson 8: Multiplication of Whole Numbers

Directions: Choose the correct answer to each equation. Choose "None of these" if the correct answer is not given.

Examples

A. 324
     x 4

  (A) 328
  (B) 1,296
  (C) 320
  (D) None of these

B. 121 x 49 =

  (F) 5,929
  (G) 72
  (H) 170
  (J) None of these

 Clue Pay close attention to the numbers in the problem and in the answer choices. If you misread even one number, you will probably choose the wrong answer.

● Practice

1. 37
    x 8

  (A) 296
  (B) 166
  (C) 45
  (D) None of these

5. 178
    x 84

  (A) 262
  (B) 94
  (C) 14,952
  (D) None of these

2. 1,751
    x 2

  (F) 1,753
  (G) 1,749
  (H) 3,502
  (J) None of these

6. □ x 4 = 72

  (F) 76
  (G) 68
  (H) 18
  (J) None of these

3. 79
    x 11

  (A) 68
  (B) 90
  (C) 869
  (D) None of these

7. 304
    x 57

  (A) 361
  (B) 247
  (C) 5 R19
  (D) None of these

4. 205
    x 4

  (F) 201
  (G) 820
  (H) 51 R4
  (J) None of these

8. 132 x □ = 528

  (F) 660
  (G) 4
  (H) 396
  (J) None of these

 STOP

Name _____   Date_____

MATH: COMPUTATION

● Lesson 9: Division of Whole Numbers

Directions: Choose the correct answer to each equation. Choose "None of these" if the correct answer is not given.

Examples

A. $42 \div 7 =$
- Ⓐ 49
- Ⓑ 294
- Ⓒ 6
- Ⓓ None of these

B. $6\overline{)445}$
- Ⓕ 63 R4
- Ⓖ 78 R1
- Ⓗ 74 R3
- Ⓙ None of these

 Clue If the correct answer is not one of the choices, mark the space for "None of these."

● Practice

1. $7\overline{)89}$
- Ⓐ 12 R 5
- Ⓑ 12
- Ⓒ 13
- Ⓓ None of these

5. $72 \div \square = 9$
- Ⓐ 63
- Ⓑ 8
- Ⓒ 648
- Ⓓ None of these

2. $40 \div 5 =$
- Ⓕ 8
- Ⓖ 35
- Ⓗ 200
- Ⓙ None of these

6. $24\overline{)964}$
- Ⓕ 23,136
- Ⓖ 40 R4
- Ⓗ 940
- Ⓙ None of these

3. $374 \div 6 =$
- Ⓐ 62 R2
- Ⓑ 2,244
- Ⓒ 368
- Ⓓ None of these

7. $15\overline{)90}$
- Ⓐ 75
- Ⓑ 6
- Ⓒ 105
- Ⓓ None of these

4. $2\overline{)19}$
- Ⓕ 38
- Ⓖ 9 R1
- Ⓗ 9
- Ⓙ None of these

8. $88 \div \square = 11$
- Ⓕ 80
- Ⓖ 8
- Ⓗ 10
- Ⓙ None of these

 STOP

MATH: COMPUTATION
SAMPLE TEST

● **Directions:** Choose the correct answer to each equation. Remember to reduce fraction answers to simplest form. Choose "None of these" if the correct answer is not given.

Examples

A. $\begin{array}{r} 145 \\ \times\ 32 \end{array}$

- (A) 4,640
- (B) 725
- (C) 177
- (D) None of these

B. $\frac{8}{9} + \frac{5}{9} + \frac{1}{9} =$

- (F) $1\frac{3}{9}$
- (G) $\frac{5}{9}$
- (H) $\frac{9}{15}$
- (J) None of these

---

1. $\begin{array}{r} 0.4 \\ -\ 0.4 \end{array}$

- (A) 0
- (B) 1.8
- (C) 1
- (D) None of these

2. $5 \times 40 =$

- (F) 240
- (G) 45
- (H) 200
- (J) None of these

3. $5{,}951 + 3{,}291 =$

- (A) 2,660
- (B) 9,242
- (C) 924.4
- (D) None of these

4. $97\overline{)488}$

- (F) 5.3
- (G) 47,336
- (H) 5 R3
- (J) None of these

5. $\begin{array}{r} 4\frac{6}{11} \\ +\ 3\frac{2}{11} \end{array}$

- (A) 8
- (B) $1\frac{4}{11}$
- (C) $7\frac{8}{11}$
- (D) None of these

6. $48 \div 4 =$

- (F) 42
- (G) 192
- (H) 12
- (J) None of these

7. $\begin{array}{r} \$6.27 \\ -\ 2.89 \end{array}$

- (A) $9.16
- (B) $3.38
- (C) $18.12
- (D) None of these

8. $879 + \square = 922$

- (F) 43
- (G) 1,801
- (H) 1.04
- (J) None of these

9. $463 - 72 =$

- (A) 391
- (B) 33,336
- (C) 535
- (D) None of these

10. $45 + 62 + 71 =$

- (F) 178
- (G) 2,790
- (H) 168
- (J) None of these

GO ON

MATH: COMPUTATION
SAMPLE TEST (cont.)

11. $12 \times 8 =$
- (A) 4
- (B) 96
- (C) 20
- (D) None of these

12. $\begin{array}{r} 78 \\ +\ 46 \end{array}$
- (F) 32
- (G) 114
- (H) 122
- (J) None of these

13. $18.2 - 9.53 =$
- (A) 8.67
- (B) 867
- (C) 86.7
- (D) None of these

14. $5\overline{)82}$
- (F) 30 R2
- (G) 36
- (H) 36 R2
- (J) None of these

15. $\begin{array}{r} 124 \\ \times\ 53 \end{array}$
- (A) 71
- (B) 177
- (C) 6,572
- (D) None of these

16. $\frac{18}{15} - \frac{9}{15} =$
- (F) $\frac{28}{15}$
- (G) $\frac{13}{15}$
- (H) $\frac{3}{5}$
- (J) None of these

17. $\begin{array}{r} 794 \\ -\ 318 \end{array}$
- (A) 476
- (B) 384
- (C) 1,112
- (D) None of these

18. $125 - \square = 106$
- (F) 231
- (G) 19
- (H) 13,250
- (J) None of these

19. $\frac{7}{10} - \frac{2}{10} =$
- (A) $\frac{9}{10}$
- (B) $\frac{1}{2}$
- (C) $\frac{14}{10}$
- (D) None of these

20. $\begin{array}{r} 2.46 \\ -\ 0.87 \end{array}$
- (F) 2.21
- (G) 3.33
- (H) 1.59
- (J) None of these

21. $1\frac{1}{2} + 1\frac{2}{2}$
- (A) $3\frac{1}{2}$
- (B) $2\frac{3}{2}$
- (C) 3
- (D) None of these

22. $\square + 16 = 81$
- (F) 5
- (G) 97
- (H) 65
- (J) None of these

STOP

Name _____ Date _____

MATH: APPLICATIONS

● Lesson 10: Geometry

Directions: Choose the correct answer for each problem and mark it.

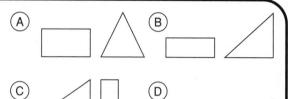

A. Kim made one straight cut across the trapezoid. Which pair of figures could be the two cut pieces of the trapezoid?

Read carefully. Look for key words, numbers, and figures before you choose an answer.

● Practice

1. The area of a rectangle is 943 square inches. The length of the rectangle is 41 inches. What is the width of the rectangle?

   Ⓐ 24 inches
   Ⓑ 32 inches
   Ⓒ 23 inches
   Ⓓ 18 inches

   41" ?

2. Which of the following letters has a line of symmetry?

   Ⓕ R
   Ⓖ W
   Ⓗ Z
   Ⓙ S

3. How many sides does a rectangle have?

   Ⓐ 0
   Ⓑ 2
   Ⓒ 3
   Ⓓ 4

4. The steering wheel on a car is most shaped like a —

   Ⓕ cube
   Ⓖ sphere
   Ⓗ square
   Ⓙ circle

GO ON

— MATH: APPLICATIONS —

● Lesson 10: Geometry (cont.)

5. **What kind of lines are shown here?**

- (A) right
- (B) parallel
- (C) perpendicular
- (D) obtuse

6. **Which of the figures below is a sphere?**

- (F)
- (G)
- (H)
- (J)

7. **How many edges does a cube have?**

- (A) 4
- (B) 6
- (C) 12
- (D) 8

8. **Which letter has a line of symmetry?**

- (F) J
- (G) S
- (H) M
- (J) Q

9. **What is the area of this shape in square units?**

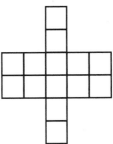

- (A) 14
- (B) 12
- (C) 22
- (D) 20

GO ON

1-57768-974-7 *Spectrum Test Practice 4*

MATH: APPLICATIONS

● Lesson 10: Geometry (cont.)

10. Dylan drew a shape with 4 sides. Two sides were the same length and one corner was 90 degrees. What shape did Dylan draw?

    (F) parallelogram
    (G) rectangle
    (H) triangle
    (J) hexagon

11. **Which pair of shapes are similar?**

    (A)

    (B)

    (C)

    (D)

12. **Which figure is symmetric?**

    (F)

    (G)

    (H)

    (J)

13. **What is the perimeter of a triangular room if all the sides are 4.5 meters long?**

    (A) 9 meters
    (B) 18 meters
    (C) 13.5 meters
    (D) 22.5 meters

14. **How many sides does a circle have?**

    (F) 12
    (G) 2
    (H) 1
    (J) 0

STOP

Name _____   Date_____

━━━━━━━━━━━━━━ **MATH: APPLICATIONS** ━━━━━━━━━━━━━━

● **Lesson 11: Measurement**

Directions: Choose the correct answer for each problem and mark it.

Examples

A.   Which unit would be best for measuring the length of a new pencil?

   Ⓐ   feet
   Ⓑ   meters
   Ⓒ   inches
   Ⓓ   liters

B.   If Marcus gave the cashier a 10-dollar bill for an $8.96 check, how much change should he get back?

   Ⓕ $11.04
   Ⓖ $2.00
   Ⓗ $1.04
   Ⓙ $18.96

 Clue   Pay close attention to the units used in each problem. If you misread, you may choose the wrong answer.

● **Practice**

1.   **Saturday   Sunday**

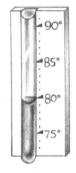 

How did the temperature change between Saturday and Sunday? On Sunday it was —

   Ⓐ   5 degrees cooler than Saturday
   Ⓑ   10 degrees cooler than Saturday
   Ⓒ   5 degrees warmer than Saturday
   Ⓓ   10 degrees warmer than Saturday

2.   **What is the perimeter of the rectangle?**

7 meters

4 meters

   Ⓕ   22 meters
   Ⓖ   18 meters
   Ⓗ   11 meters
   Ⓙ   3 meters

3.   **How many liters are in one kiloliter?**

   Ⓐ   10
   Ⓑ   1
   Ⓒ   100
   Ⓓ   1,000

4.   **Rachelle started her homework at 3:00. She finished at 5:15. For how long did she work?**

   Ⓕ   3 hours
   Ⓖ   2 hours
   Ⓗ   140 minutes
   Ⓙ   2 hours, 15 minutes

GO ON

● Lesson 11: Measurement (cont.)

5. **What temperature does this thermometer show?**

   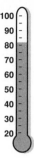

   Ⓐ 87° F
   Ⓑ 82° F
   Ⓒ 80° F
   Ⓓ 78° F

6. **Angela saved her allowance to buy a new pair of sneakers. She had $70.00. After buying the sneakers, how much money did she have left?**

   Ⓕ $9.25
   Ⓖ $8.75
   Ⓗ $7.65
   Ⓙ Not enough information

7. **The school fair starts the Tuesday after school ends. If school ends on Friday, May 30, on what date does the school fair begin?**

   Ⓐ May 31
   Ⓑ June 1
   Ⓒ June 2
   Ⓓ June 3

SUN	MON	TUE	WED	THUR	FRI	SAT
				1	2	3
4	5	6	7	8	9	10
11	12	13	14	15	16	17
18	19	20	21	22	23	24
25	26	27	28	29	30	31

8. **Scott ran 1 mile in 7 minutes and 42 seconds at the start of the track season. By the end of the track season, Scott could run 1 mile in 6 minutes and 37 seconds. How much time did Scott cut off his running time?**

   Ⓕ 1 minute, 3 seconds
   Ⓖ 1 minute, 9 seconds
   Ⓗ 5 seconds
   Ⓙ None of these

9. **3 yards is —**

   Ⓐ 24 feet
   Ⓑ 32 feet
   Ⓒ 36 feet
   Ⓓ None of these

10. **Leslie is making punch in a very large punch bowl. Orange juice comes in different-sized containers. Which size container should she buy in order to purchase the fewest number of containers?**

    Ⓕ a one-cup container
    Ⓖ a one-gallon container
    Ⓗ a one-pint container
    Ⓙ a one-quart container

11. **How many hours are in a week?**

    Ⓐ 84 hours
    Ⓑ 168 hours
    Ⓒ 60 hours
    Ⓓ 336 hours

12. **Which of these would you probably use to measure a person's waist?**

    Ⓕ meter stick
    Ⓖ tape measure
    Ⓗ yardstick
    Ⓙ ruler

Name _____ Date _____

● **Lesson 11: Measurement (cont.)**

13. **You have coins that total $0.71. What coins do you have?**

    (A) 3 dimes, 1 nickel, 1 penny

    (B) 1 quarter, 3 dimes, 1 penny

    (C) 2 quarters, 1 dime, 1 nickel, 1 penny

    (D) 2 quarters, 2 dimes, 1 penny

14. **What time does this clock show?**

    (F) 8:52

    (G) 9:52

    (H) 10:52

    (J) None of these

15. **Which of the following shows 25 minutes to eight o'clock?**

    (A) 8:25

    (B) 7:40

    (C) 6:35

    (D) 7:35

16. **You are mailing in your brother's college application today. It is a regular letter size. You must make sure you have enough postage. How much do you think it weighs?**

    (F) 1 pound

    (G) 8 pounds

    (H) 1 ounce

    (J) 8 ounces

17. **It is 6:00 now and the movie starts in 40 minutes. What time will it be then?**

    (A)    (B)

    (C)    (D)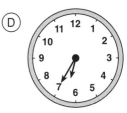

18. **If Nick has a water bottle that holds 2 gallons, which of the following would fill it?**

    (F) 4 cups

    (G) 3 pints

    (H) 8 quarts

    (J) 1 liter

19. **Which of the following would you probably measure in feet?**

    (A) length of a pencil

    (B) distance between two cities

    (C) amount of juice left in a bottle

    (D) the length of a couch

20. **5 kilograms is equal to —**

    (F) 5 dekagrams

    (G) 500 grams

    (H) 50 grams

    (J) 5,000 grams

GO ON

● Lesson 11: Measurement (cont.)

21. Toby left his house for school at 7:35 A.M. He arrived at school at 7:50 A.M. How many minutes did it take Toby to get to school?

- (A) 15 minutes
- (B) 20 minutes
- (C) 25 minutes
- (D) 10 minutes

22. How many feet are there in one mile?

- (F) 5,028 feet
- (G) 5,280 feet
- (H) 5,820 feet
- (J) 8,520 feet

23. Renee measured her garden, and it is between 5 and 6 yards long. About how many feet and inches is it?

- (A) 101 feet
- (B) 15 feet
- (C) 15 feet 11 inches
- (D) 18 feet 1 inch

24. What temperature will this thermometer show if the temperature rises 10°?

- (F) 32°
- (G) 35°
- (H) 55°
- (J) 43°

25. Phong buys a new sweatshirt for $15.48. He pays with 1 ten-dollar, 1 five-dollar, and 1 one-dollar bill. How much change will he get back?

- (A) $0.48
- (B) $1.00
- (C) $52
- (D) $0.52

26. How many ounces are in 1 pound?

- (F) 6 ounces
- (G) 8 ounces
- (H) 16 ounces
- (J) 32 ounces

27. What is the length of this line to the nearest half centimeter?

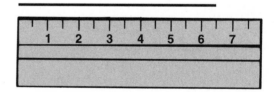

- (A) 6 cm
- (B) 3.5 cm
- (C) 7.1 cm
- (D) 6.5 cm

STOP

Name _____   Date_____

MATH: APPLICATIONS

● Lesson 12: Problem Solving

Directions: Read and work each problem. Choose the correct answer and mark it.

Example

A. A store has 3,802 compact discs on the shelves. The store receives 2 new cases of compact discs. There are 320 compact discs in each case. How many compact discs does the store have now?

- (A) 640 compact discs
- (B) 3,802 compact discs
- (C) 4,442 compact discs
- (D) 3,482 compact discs

 Clue Read all the answers before choosing one. Reread a problem if you don't understand it.

● Practice

1. Grant went to get a frozen yogurt from the concession stand. He could choose vanilla, chocolate, or twist yogurt. He could have a cup, wafer cone, or sugar cone. How many possible combinations does Grant have?

- (A) 6
- (B) 3
- (C) 8
- (D) 9

2. How many more tickets were sold on Friday than on Tuesday?

```
CENTER CINEMAS
MOVIE TICKET SALES

MONDAY
TUESDAY
WEDNESDAY
THURSDAY
FRIDAY

KEY: 10 TICKETS =
```

- (F) 45
- (G) 55
- (H) 75
- (J) 295

3. If you wanted to compare the features of two different solid shapes, the best thing to use would be a —

- (A) Venn diagram
- (B) pie chart
- (C) tally chart
- (D) line graph

4. Larry, Carey, and Harry went out for lunch. Each friend ordered a salad. The choices were egg, tuna, and chicken. Carey won't eat egg. Larry never orders tuna. Harry only likes chicken. Each friend ate something different. Who ordered tuna?

- (F) Larry
- (G) Carey
- (H) Harry
- (J) Not enough information

 GO ON

MATH: APPLICATIONS

● Lesson 12: Problem Solving (cont.)

5. Giraffes and birds are drinking at a watering hole. There are 10 animals with a total of 30 legs there. How many 2-legged birds are there? How many 4-legged giraffes are there?

   (A) 5 birds, 5 giraffes
   (B) 4 birds, 3 giraffes
   (C) 2 birds, 5 giraffes
   (D) 6 birds, 1 giraffe

6. The school basketball team scored a total of 1,148 points during 28 games in the season. What was the average number of points scored per game?

   (F) 47
   (G) 1,120
   (H) 40
   (J) None of these

7. Which type of graph would be best to show how the average weekly temperature changed in one town from month to month?

   (A) pie chart
   (B) tally chart
   (C) bar graph
   (D) line graph

Use the graph below to answer the questions that follow.

Favorite Vacation Destination

beach	🕶 🕶 🕶 🕶
water park	🕶 🕶 🕶 🕶 🕶
amusement park	🕶 🕶 🕶 🕶 🕶 🕶

Key: 🕶 = 8 votes

8. For how many votes does one symbol stand?

   (F) 2
   (G) 5
   (H) 6
   (J) 8

9. How many people answered this survey?

   (A) $14\frac{1}{2}$
   (B) 72
   (C) 148
   (D) None of these

10. How many more people would rather go to an amusement park than the beach?

   (F) 10
   (G) 12
   (H) 20
   (J) 22

GO ON

MATH: APPLICATIONS

● **Lesson 12: Problem Solving (cont.)**

11. Aijuin used $\frac{1}{8}$ of a stick of butter to make muffins. She then used $\frac{2}{3}$ of a cup of flour to make bread. How much butter did she use in the muffins and bread?

    Ⓐ $\frac{1}{8}$ stick

    Ⓑ 1.4 stick

    Ⓒ $\frac{2}{3}$ stick

    Ⓓ Not enough information

12. Sara has a piece of ribbon that is 60 inches long. She will use $\frac{2}{3}$ of the ribbon to make bows. If the answer to this problem is 20 inches, what is the question?

    Ⓕ How much ribbon did she use?

    Ⓖ How much ribbon is left over?

    Ⓗ How much is $\frac{2}{3}$?

    Ⓙ How many bows does she make?

13. There were 488 balloons decorating the gymnasium for a party. There were 97 students at the party. If each student brought home an equal number of balloons after the party, how many balloons were left over?

    Ⓐ 3 balloons

    Ⓑ 46 balloons

    Ⓒ 12 balloons

    Ⓓ None of these

14. If you burn 318 calories in 60 minutes of playing tennis, how many calories would you burn in 30 minutes?

    Ⓕ 159 calories

    Ⓖ 636 calories

    Ⓗ 258 calories

    Ⓙ 288 calories

15. There are 62 students on a class trip. They are taking a bus to the nature park. The ride to the park takes 25 minutes and the ride home takes 30 minutes. Lunch at the park costs $3.25 per child. How much money do the students spend to get into the park?

    Ⓐ $201.50

    Ⓑ $50.00

    Ⓒ $120.25

    Ⓓ Not enough information

16. The school play sold out every night. The play ran for 3 nights, and 345 people attended each night. Tickets cost $4.25 each. How much money did the school play make?

    Ⓕ $1,239.50

    Ⓖ $1,466.25

    Ⓗ $1,035.00

    Ⓙ $4,398.75

GO ON

MATH: APPLICATIONS

● Lesson 12: Problem Solving (cont.)

The fourth grade students at Zinser Elementary were asked to do reports on one of the following five birds: hummingbird, hawk, owl, blue jay, or California condor. Use the graph below to answer the questions that follow.

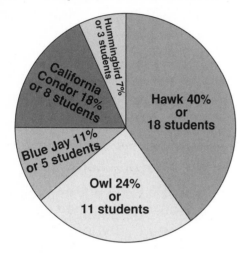

17. How many fourth graders are at Zinser Elementary?

(A) 100

(B) 45

(C) 47

(D) 50

18. Which of the following lists the birds from least to greatest favorite?

(F) hawk, owl, California condor, blue jay, hummingbird

(G) blue jay, hummingbird, California condor, owl, hawk

(H) hummingbird, blue jay, California condor, owl, hawk

(J) California condor, hawk, owl, blue jay, hummingbird

19. Which two birds combined get more than 50 percent of the vote?

(A) hawk and owl

(B) hummingbird and California condor

(C) hummingbird and blue jay

(D) hawk and hummingbird

20. What percent of the vote do the hummingbird, California condor, and blue jay make up together?

(F) 40%

(G) 25%

(H) 30%

(J) 36%

STOP

Name _____   Date _____

MATH: APPLICATIONS
SAMPLE TEST

● **Directions:** Read and work each problem. Choose the correct answer and mark it.

Examples

A. Jesse bought a pack of cards for $1.25 and a baseball for $8.39. He has $5.36 left over. With how much money did he start?

- Ⓐ $20.00
- Ⓑ $9.64
- Ⓒ $1.78
- Ⓓ $15.00

B. Which of the following letters is symmetrical?

- Ⓕ Z
- Ⓖ S
- Ⓗ R
- Ⓙ Y

1. Aidan bought a slice of pizza and a soda at the arcade. The pizza cost $4.50, and the soda cost $2.75. Aidan paid with a 10-dollar bill. How much change did he receive?

- Ⓐ $5.50
- Ⓑ $3.00
- Ⓒ $2.75
- Ⓓ $7.25

2. If 1 pound of potatoes costs $2.60, and Miko needs to buy 8 pounds to make potato salad, what formula would she use to find the total cost?

- Ⓕ $2.60 + 8 = ☐
- Ⓖ 8 – $2.60 = ☐
- Ⓗ $2.60 x 8 = ☐
- Ⓙ 8 ÷ $2.60 = ☐

3. Which of these has the greatest volume?

- Ⓐ 4 quarts
- Ⓑ 2 gallons
- Ⓒ 8 pints
- Ⓓ 17 cups

4. Which of the following directions could be used to move from zero to point A on the grid below?

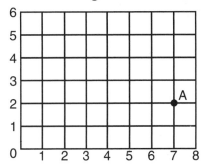

- Ⓕ Go right 7 units and up 2 units.
- Ⓖ Go right 6 units and up 1 unit.
- Ⓗ Go right 8 units and up 2 units.
- Ⓙ Go up 4 units and right 7 units.

5. Which of the following is not shaped like a sphere?

- Ⓐ basketball
- Ⓑ beach ball
- Ⓒ hockey puck
- Ⓓ golf ball

GO ON

MATH: APPLICATIONS
SAMPLE TEST (cont.)

6. What is the area of this shape?

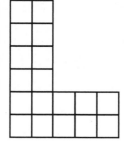

- (F) 16 square units
- (G) 20 square units
- (H) 22 square units
- (J) 18 square units

7. If Jerry walked 2 miles for charity, how many feet did he walk?

- (A) 20 feet
- (B) 6 feet
- (C) 3,520 feet
- (D) 10,560 feet

8. How many sides does a hexagon have?

- (F) 5
- (G) 6
- (H) 7
- (J) 8

9. Sara wants to measure how much applesauce she made this fall. If she uses metric, which unit should she use?

- (A) gram
- (B) liter
- (C) kilogram
- (D) centimeter

10. A sailboat takes 124 passengers on a cruise on a lake. If the sailboat makes 53 tours a month, how many people ride on the boat each month?

- (F) 5,789 people
- (G) 5,499 people
- (H) 6,845 people
- (J) 6,572 people

11. Which of the following thermometers shows that it is 67° F?

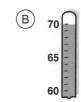

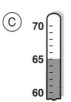

12. Which line segment is congruent to AB?

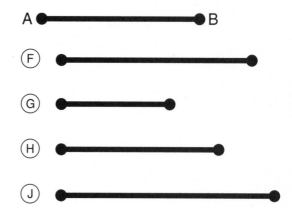

13. Terrance collected 468 seashells in 18 visits to the beach. How many seashells did he collect during each visit?

- (A) 29
- (B) 26
- (C) 32
- (D) 23

14. A truck driver makes 23 trips each month. Each trip is 576 miles long. How many miles does the truck driver travel in a month?

   (F) 13,248 miles
   (G) 12,248 miles
   (H) 13,589 miles
   (J) 14,553 miles

15. A gas station sells an average of 847 gallons of gasoline per day. How many gallons will be sold in a year?

   (A) 309,155 gallons
   (B) 847 gallons
   (C) 321,860 gallons
   (D) Not enough information

16. What is the perimeter of this figure?

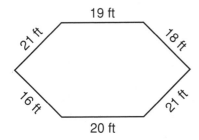

   (F) 95 feet
   (G) 380 feet
   (H) 115 feet
   (J) 420 feet

17. 4 minutes =
   (A) 120 seconds
   (B) 240 seconds
   (C) 360 seconds
   (D) 480 seconds

18. A store manager ordered 4 cases of juice boxes. There are 6 boxes in each package and 12 packages in a case. How many juice boxes did he order altogether?

   (F) 24 boxes
   (G) 288 boxes
   (H) 48 boxes
   (J) Not enough information

19. Which of the following shows a correct line of symmetry?

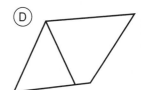
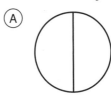

20. If it is 3:30 now, what time was it 20 minutes ago?

GO ON

MATH: APPLICATIONS
SAMPLE TEST (cont.)

Study the graph. Use the information to answer items 21–23.

Top Countries Generating Hydroelectric Power

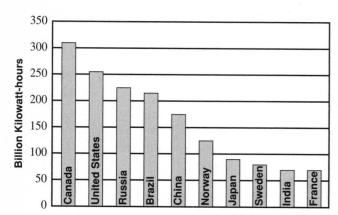

21. **Which country produces more hydroelectricity than the United States?**

    Ⓐ Brazil

    Ⓑ China

    Ⓒ Canada

    Ⓓ India

22. **Which country produces more hydroelectricity than Brazil and less than the United States?**

    Ⓕ Russia

    Ⓖ China

    Ⓗ Canada

    Ⓙ Brazil

23. **Which two countries produce about the same amount of hydroelectricity?**

    Ⓐ India and France

    Ⓑ Russia and Brazil

    Ⓒ Japan and Sweden

    Ⓓ Sweden and India

Study the graph. Use the information to answer items 24–26.

Cheese Production
Percent by Type, 1 Year's Production

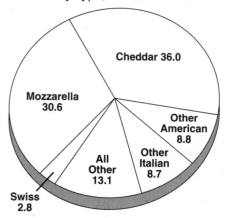

24. **Which cheese is made the least?**

    Ⓕ Other Italian

    Ⓖ Mozzarella

    Ⓗ Cheddar

    Ⓙ Swiss

25. **Which two cheeses together make up 66.6 percent of the year's production?**

    Ⓐ Other American and Other Italian

    Ⓑ Cheddar and Mozzarella

    Ⓒ Mozzarella and Swiss

    Ⓓ Cheddar and Swiss

26. **What percent of cheese production is made up of cheeses other than Cheddar and Mozzarella?**

    Ⓕ 33.4%

    Ⓖ 30%

    Ⓗ 66.6%

    Ⓙ 8.8%

STOP

ANSWER SHEET

STUDENT'S NAME

LAST	FIRST	MI

(Letter bubble grid A–Z for name fields)

SCHOOL

TEACHER

FEMALE ◯   MALE ◯

BIRTH DATE

MONTH	DAY	YEAR
JAN ◯	0 0	0
FEB ◯	1 1	1
MAR ◯	2 2	2
APR ◯	3 3	3
MAY ◯	4	4
JUN ◯	5	5 5
JUL ◯	6	6 6
AUG ◯	7	7 7
SEP ◯	8	8 8
OCT ◯	9	9 9
NOV ◯		0
DEC ◯		

GRADE

③   ④   ⑤

Part 1: CONCEPTS

A Ⓐ Ⓑ Ⓒ Ⓓ
B Ⓕ Ⓖ Ⓗ Ⓙ

1 Ⓐ Ⓑ Ⓒ Ⓓ
2 Ⓕ Ⓖ Ⓗ Ⓙ
3 Ⓐ Ⓑ Ⓒ Ⓓ
4 Ⓕ Ⓖ Ⓗ Ⓙ
5 Ⓐ Ⓑ Ⓒ Ⓓ
6 Ⓕ Ⓖ Ⓗ Ⓙ
7 Ⓐ Ⓑ Ⓒ Ⓓ
8 Ⓕ Ⓖ Ⓗ Ⓙ
9 Ⓐ Ⓑ Ⓒ Ⓓ
10 Ⓕ Ⓖ Ⓗ Ⓙ
11 Ⓐ Ⓑ Ⓒ Ⓓ
12 Ⓕ Ⓖ Ⓗ Ⓙ
13 Ⓐ Ⓑ Ⓒ Ⓓ
14 Ⓕ Ⓖ Ⓗ Ⓙ
15 Ⓐ Ⓑ Ⓒ Ⓓ
16 Ⓕ Ⓖ Ⓗ Ⓙ
17 Ⓐ Ⓑ Ⓒ Ⓓ
18 Ⓕ Ⓖ Ⓗ Ⓙ
19 Ⓐ Ⓑ Ⓒ Ⓓ
20 Ⓕ Ⓖ Ⓗ Ⓙ
21 Ⓐ Ⓑ Ⓒ Ⓓ

Part 2: COMPUTATION

A Ⓐ Ⓑ Ⓒ Ⓓ
B Ⓕ Ⓖ Ⓗ Ⓙ

1 Ⓐ Ⓑ Ⓒ Ⓓ
2 Ⓕ Ⓖ Ⓗ Ⓙ
3 Ⓐ Ⓑ Ⓒ Ⓓ
4 Ⓕ Ⓖ Ⓗ Ⓙ
5 Ⓐ Ⓑ Ⓒ Ⓓ
6 Ⓕ Ⓖ Ⓗ Ⓙ
7 Ⓐ Ⓑ Ⓒ Ⓓ
8 Ⓕ Ⓖ Ⓗ Ⓙ
9 Ⓐ Ⓑ Ⓒ Ⓓ
10 Ⓕ Ⓖ Ⓗ Ⓙ
11 Ⓐ Ⓑ Ⓒ Ⓓ
12 Ⓕ Ⓖ Ⓗ Ⓙ
13 Ⓐ Ⓑ Ⓒ Ⓓ
14 Ⓕ Ⓖ Ⓗ Ⓙ
15 Ⓐ Ⓑ Ⓒ Ⓓ
16 Ⓕ Ⓖ Ⓗ Ⓙ
17 Ⓐ Ⓑ Ⓒ Ⓓ
18 Ⓕ Ⓖ Ⓗ Ⓙ
19 Ⓐ Ⓑ Ⓒ Ⓓ
20 Ⓕ Ⓖ Ⓗ Ⓙ
21 Ⓐ Ⓑ Ⓒ Ⓓ
22 Ⓕ Ⓖ Ⓗ Ⓙ

Part 3: APPLICATIONS

A Ⓐ Ⓑ Ⓒ Ⓓ

1 Ⓐ Ⓑ Ⓒ Ⓓ
2 Ⓕ Ⓖ Ⓗ Ⓙ
3 Ⓐ Ⓑ Ⓒ Ⓓ
4 Ⓕ Ⓖ Ⓗ Ⓙ
5 Ⓐ Ⓑ Ⓒ Ⓓ
6 Ⓕ Ⓖ Ⓗ Ⓙ
7 Ⓐ Ⓑ Ⓒ Ⓓ
8 Ⓕ Ⓖ Ⓗ Ⓙ
9 Ⓐ Ⓑ Ⓒ Ⓓ
10 Ⓕ Ⓖ Ⓗ Ⓙ
11 Ⓐ Ⓑ Ⓒ Ⓓ
12 Ⓕ Ⓖ Ⓗ Ⓙ
13 Ⓐ Ⓑ Ⓒ Ⓓ
14 Ⓕ Ⓖ Ⓗ Ⓙ
15 Ⓐ Ⓑ Ⓒ Ⓓ
16 Ⓕ Ⓖ Ⓗ Ⓙ
17 Ⓐ Ⓑ Ⓒ Ⓓ
18 Ⓕ Ⓖ Ⓗ Ⓙ
19 Ⓐ Ⓑ Ⓒ Ⓓ
20 Ⓕ Ⓖ Ⓗ Ⓙ
21 Ⓐ Ⓑ Ⓒ Ⓓ
22 Ⓕ Ⓖ Ⓗ Ⓙ
23 Ⓐ Ⓑ Ⓒ Ⓓ
24 Ⓕ Ⓖ Ⓗ Ⓙ
25 Ⓐ Ⓑ Ⓒ Ⓓ
26 Ⓕ Ⓖ Ⓗ Ⓙ
27 Ⓐ Ⓑ Ⓒ Ⓓ

1-57768-974-7 Spectrum Test Practice 4

MATH PRACTICE TEST

● Part 1: Concepts

Directions: Read and work each problem. Show each fraction in simplest form. Choose the correct answer and mark it.

Examples

A. What number is missing from the sequence shown below?

64, 55, 46, ___, 28, 19

- (A) 37
- (B) 36
- (C) 30
- (D) 34

B. What is the correct standard form for 10,000,000 + 8,000,000 + 400,000 + 30,000 + 4,000 + 900 + 4?

- (F) 18,434
- (G) 18,434,904
- (H) 180,434,904
- (J) 18,434,940

---

1. Mark is selling chocolate bars for the school band. He sells 2 on the first day, 6 on the second day, and 10 on the third day. If this pattern continues, how many will he sell on the fourth day?

- (A) 20
- (B) 18
- (C) 12
- (D) 14

2. Which of these is a group of odd numbers?

- (F) 17, 19, 25, 99
- (G) 5, 14, 23, 67
- (H) 13, 16, 19, 21
- (J) 6, 35, 48, 98

3. What number goes in the box to make this number sentence true?

$$\frac{\square}{2} = \frac{2}{4}$$

- (A) 0
- (B) 4
- (C) 1
- (D) 2

4. How many thousands are in 1,000,000?

- (F) 10,000
- (G) 1,000,000
- (H) 100
- (J) 1,000

5. What should replace the □ in the number sentence below?

7 □ 6 = 42

- (A) +
- (B) −
- (C) x
- (D) ÷

6. A number rounded to the nearest ten is 350. When it is rounded to the nearest hundred, the number becomes 400. What is the number?

- (F) 349
- (G) 359
- (H) 353
- (J) 345

GO ON

MATH PRACTICE TEST
Part 1: Concepts (cont.)

7. What fraction of the shape below is shaded?

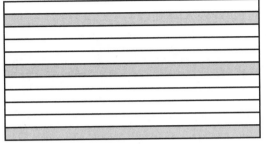

   (A) $\frac{3}{10}$

   (B) $\frac{3}{11}$

   (C) $\frac{1}{3}$

   (D) $\frac{2}{3}$

8. Which of these numerals has a 6 in the hundreds place?

   (F) 11,610

   (G) 10,006

   (H) 6,313

   (J) 16,452

9. Which numeral fits in this number sentence to make it true?

   (A) 12

   (B) 3 $24 - \square = 8$

   (C) 16

   (D) 14

10. Which of the following is the closest estimate for the equation?

   (F) 700

   (G) 600 $358 \times 2 = \square$

   (H) 900

   (J) 400

11. What is another way to write 45 thousands?

   (A) 450,000

   (B) 45,000

   (C) 450

   (D) 4,500

12. Which decimal below names the smallest number?

   (F) 0.06

   (G) 0.6

   (H) 0.64

   (J) 0.064

13. What is the correct sign to complete the equation below?

   (A) = $426.10 \square \ $416.19

   (B) <

   (C) >

   (D) None of these

14. Which of these has a greater value than $\frac{1}{8}$?

   (F) $\frac{1}{18}$

   (G) $\frac{1}{16}$

   (H) $\frac{1}{6}$

   (J) $\frac{1}{32}$

GO ON

15. What is the value of the underlined digit?

    9,439

    Ⓐ forty
    Ⓑ four thousand
    Ⓒ four hundred
    Ⓓ four

16. The function table below shows input and output numbers. The rule used to change the numbers is shown. What number completes the table?

    Rule: Multiply by 2, then add 7.

IN	OUT
3	13
4	?
5	17

    Ⓕ 14
    Ⓖ 16
    Ⓗ 15
    Ⓙ None of these

17. Which number in $1.62 would you look at to round it to the nearest dollar?

    Ⓐ 1
    Ⓑ 6
    Ⓒ 2
    Ⓓ None of these

18. The soccer team had $9\frac{1}{2}$ feet of submarine sandwich for their party. They ate 7 feet. Which equation below would you use to find out how much sandwich they had left?

    Ⓕ $9\frac{1}{2} + 7 = \square$
    Ⓖ $9\frac{1}{2} - 7 = \square$
    Ⓗ $9\frac{1}{2} \times 7 = \square$
    Ⓙ $9\frac{1}{2} \div 7 = \square$

19. Which shows the numbers ordered from greatest to least?

    Ⓐ 5,693; 6,432; 43,534; 710,002
    Ⓑ 14,632; 346; 123,152; 9,965
    Ⓒ 711,002; 182,976; 6,234; 1,624
    Ⓓ 643,342; 72,816; 143,524; 9,569

20. 0.59 =

    Ⓕ $\frac{5}{9}$
    Ⓖ $\frac{590}{100}$
    Ⓗ $\frac{59}{100}$
    Ⓙ $\frac{59}{10}$

21. Which of the following number facts does not belong to the same family or group as $35 \div 7 = 5$?

    Ⓐ $7 \times 5 = 35$
    Ⓑ $35 \div 5 = 7$
    Ⓒ $5 \times 7 = 35$
    Ⓓ $5 + 7 = 12$

STOP

MATH PRACTICE TEST

● Part 2: Computation

Directions: Choose the correct answer to each problem. Remember to reduce fraction answers to simplest form. Choose "None of these" if the correct answer is not given.

Examples

A. $14 \times 7 =$
- Ⓐ 21
- Ⓑ 98
- Ⓒ 7
- Ⓓ None of these

B.
$$\begin{array}{r} 26.16 \\ -\ 8.00 \end{array}$$
- Ⓕ 18.16
- Ⓖ 34.16
- Ⓗ 26.08
- Ⓙ None of these

1.
$$\begin{array}{r} 132 \\ \times\ 4 \end{array}$$
- Ⓐ 528
- Ⓑ 136
- Ⓒ 478
- Ⓓ None of these

2. $1\frac{2}{4} - \frac{3}{4}$
- Ⓕ $1\frac{5}{4}$
- Ⓖ $\frac{3}{4}$
- Ⓗ $2\frac{1}{4}$
- Ⓙ None of these

3. $\square + 6 = 44$
- Ⓐ 38
- Ⓑ 50
- Ⓒ 264
- Ⓓ None of these

4. $3\overline{)90}$
- Ⓕ 3
- Ⓖ 180
- Ⓗ 30
- Ⓙ None of these

5. $2 \times 5 \times 9 =$
- Ⓐ 16
- Ⓑ 19
- Ⓒ 91
- Ⓓ None of these

6. $5\overline{)473}$
- Ⓕ 94.3
- Ⓖ 94
- Ⓗ 94 R3
- Ⓙ None of these

7.
$$\begin{array}{r} \frac{3}{9} \\ \frac{2}{9} \\ + \end{array}$$
- Ⓐ $\frac{1}{9}$
- Ⓑ $\frac{5}{9}$
- Ⓒ $\frac{6}{9}$
- Ⓓ None of these

8. $12 \times \square = 144$
- Ⓕ 132
- Ⓖ 1,728
- Ⓗ 12
- Ⓙ None of these

9.
$$\begin{array}{r} \$0.12 \\ 4.69 \\ +\ 5.87 \end{array}$$
- Ⓐ 10.68
- Ⓑ $10.12
- Ⓒ $10.68
- Ⓓ None of these

10.
$$\begin{array}{r} 245 \\ +\ 127 \end{array}$$
- Ⓕ 372
- Ⓖ 118
- Ⓗ 3.72
- Ⓙ None of these

GO ON

Name _____   Date _____

11. $\frac{3}{8} + \frac{6}{8} =$

(A) $\frac{3}{8}$

(B) $1\frac{1}{8}$

(C) $\frac{9}{8}$

(D) None of these

17. $1\frac{5}{6}$
   $-\ \frac{6}{6}$

(A) $2\frac{5}{6}$

(B) $\frac{5}{6}$

(C) $1\frac{11}{6}$

(D) None of these

12.   757
   $-\ 129$

(F) 6.28

(G) 886

(H) 628

(J) None of these

18. $77 - \square = 43$

(F) 120

(G) 43

(H) 34

(J) None of these

13. $8,941 + 1,278 =$

(A) 9,219

(B) 10, 119

(C) 10,219

(D) None of these

19. $8\overline{)78}$

(A) 86

(B) 8

(C) 9

(D) None of these

14. $4\overline{)369}$

(F) 92

(G) 92 R1

(H) .92

(J) None of these

20. $7.00
   $-\ 2.48$

(F) $4.52

(G) $9.48

(H) 9.48

(J) None of these

15.   46
   x 82

(A) 3,772

(B) 3,672

(C) 128

(D) None of these

21.   2.5
   $+\ 1.5$

(A) 1.5

(B) 3.0

(C) 3.5

(D) None of these

16. $67 \times 6 =$

(F) 402

(G) 420

(H) 73

(J) None of these

22. $41 + \square = 96$

(F) 137

(G) 55

(H) 56

(J) None of these

STOP

Name _____   Date_____

MATH PRACTICE TEST

● Part 3: Applications

Directions: Read and work each problem. Choose the correct answer and mark it.

Example

A. Wendy is trying to figure out the area of her desk. The length is 25 inches and the width is 48 inches. What is the area of Wendy's desk?

Ⓐ 1,200 square inches
Ⓑ 1,125 square inches
Ⓒ 73 square inches
Ⓓ None of these

1. Mona started her chores at 3:30 P.M. She needed to take out the garbage, wash the dishes, water the houseplants, feed the dog, and clean up her room. Mona finished her chores just as her dad came home at 5:20 P.M. How long did it take Mona to do her chores?

Ⓐ 50 minutes
Ⓑ 2 hours
Ⓒ 1 hour, 50 minutes
Ⓓ None of these

2. Which of the following directions could be used to move from zero to point Y on the graph below?

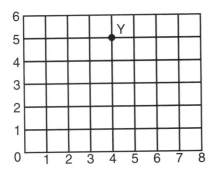

Ⓕ Go over 4 units and up 1 unit.
Ⓖ Go over 3 units and up 5 units.
Ⓗ Go over 5 units and up 4 units.
Ⓙ Go over 4 units and up 5 units.

3. If the temperature in the morning is 56° F, what will the temperature be when it rises 25° F this afternoon?

Ⓐ 78° F
Ⓑ 76° F
Ⓒ 81° F
Ⓓ 85° F

4. Which of these shapes has an area of 20 square units?

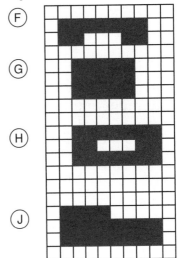

5. What is the value of 1 nickel, 2 dimes, 1 quarter, and 1 penny?

Ⓐ $0.56
Ⓑ $0.50
Ⓒ $0.51
Ⓓ $0.57

GO ON ⇨

1-57768-974-7 *Spectrum Test Practice 4*

MATH PRACTICE TEST
Part 3: Applications (cont.)

6. If each 😊 stands for 3 people, how would you show 12 people?

   F 😊 😊

   G 😊 😊 😊 😊

   H 😊 😊 😊 😊 😊

   J None of these

7. A chicken pot pie was cut into 8 slices. For dinner, the Wilsons ate $\frac{3}{8}$ of the pie. For lunch, the Wilsons ate $\frac{1}{4}$ of the pie. How much of the pie was eaten in all?

   A $\frac{5}{8}$

   B $\frac{2}{8}$

   C $\frac{4}{12}$

   D $\frac{1}{3}$

8. What is the perimeter of a rectangle with sides 20 mm and 10 mm long?

   F 30 mm
   G 50 mm
   H 60 mm
   J 200 mm

9. About how much does the container probably hold?

   A 1 gallon
   B 1 quart
   C 2 pints
   D 2 cups

10. Jean used 8 liters of water when she washed her hands and face. How many milliliters of water did she use?

    F 8,000 mL
    G 80 mL
    H 800 mL
    J 80,000 mL

11. David scored 1,832 points on a video game. Susan scored 2 times more than David. Paul scored 234 points less than Susan. What was Paul's score?

    A 3,320 points
    B 3,664 points
    C 3,430 points
    D 468 points

12. Which of the following shows parallel lines?

    F

    G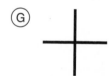

    H

    J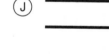

13. Which of the following letters is symmetrical?

    A E
    B D
    C A
    D Q

GO ON

MATH PRACTICE TEST
Part 3: Applications (cont.)

14. Lynda went to school at 8:00 in the morning. She had soccer practice after school for $1\frac{1}{2}$ hours. What time did Lynda get home in the evening?

- (F) 5:30
- (G) 9:30
- (H) 4:00
- (J) Not enough information

15. What is the least favorite pet in Ms. Sheely's class?

- (A) dog
- (B) cat
- (C) gerbil
- (D) fish

DOG	CAT	GERBIL	FISH

16. Rosendo and his sister combine their money to buy a new game. Rosendo has $7.48 and his sister has $8.31. How much money do they have in all?

- (F) $0.83
- (G) $15.79
- (H) $16.89
- (J) Not enough information

17. One tablespoon holds about 15 milliliters. About how many tablespoons of soup are in a 225-milliliter can?

- (A) 45 tablespoons
- (B) 5 tablespoons
- (C) 3,375 tablespoons
- (D) 15 tablespoons

18. There are 21 fish in every square yard of water in a lake. If the lake is 812 square yards, how many fish are in the lake?

- (F) 17,052
- (G) 23,708
- (H) 29,987
- (J) 14,879

19. What is the temperature in Celsius shown on this thermometer?

- (A) 75° F
- (B) 20° C
- (C) 25° C
- (D) 70° F

20. A machine makes 188 parts per hour. At that rate, how many parts can be made in 8 hours?

- (F) 1,504 parts
- (G) $23\frac{1}{2}$ parts
- (H) 180 parts
- (J) 196 parts

21. Marin starts her school sale on the Sunday of the first full week in May. The sale lasts for 2 weeks and 3 days. On what day must Marin turn in her sales slip?

- (A) Monday
- (B) Tuesday
- (C) Wednesday
- (D) Thursday

MAY						
SUN	MON	TUE	WED	THUR	FRI	SAT
			1	2	3	4
5	6	7	8	9	10	11
12	13	14	15	16	17	18
19	20	21	22	23	24	25
26	27	28	29	30	31	

GO ON

Name _____ Date _____

MATH PRACTICE TEST
Part 3: Applications (cont.)

Use the graph below to answer the questions that follow.

Favorite Flavors of Ice Cream

KEY

4th Graders

5th Graders

22. **What is the most popular ice cream flavor overall?**

  (F) vanilla

  (G) chocolate

  (H) mint

  (J) vanilla and chocolate

23. **How many fourth graders took part in this survey?**

  (A) 20

  (B) 30

  (C) 40

  (D) 50

24. **The two grade levels didn't always agree about flavor preference. On which two flavors did their answers differ the most?**

  (F) vanilla and chocolate

  (G) vanilla and mint

  (H) chocolate and mint

  (J) Not enough information

Use the graph below to answer the questions that follow.

Number of Students at Highview School

Grade Level	Number of Students
Kindergarten	𝝠𝝠𝝠𝝠𝝠𝝠𝝠𝝠
1st Grade	𝝠𝝠𝝠𝝠𝝠𝝠𝝠𝝠𝝠𝝠𝝠
2nd Grade	𝝠𝝠𝝠𝝠𝝠𝝠𝝠
3rd Grade	𝝠𝝠𝝠𝝠𝝠𝝠𝝠𝝠
4th Grade	𝝠𝝠𝝠𝝠𝝠𝝠𝝠𝝠𝝠𝝠𝝠
5th Grade	𝝠𝝠𝝠𝝠𝝠𝝠𝝠

Key: 𝝠 = 5 students

25. **How many students attend Highview School all together?**

  (A) 285

  (B) 275

  (C) 750

  (D) 290

26. **How many more students are in fourth grade than in fifth grade?**

  (F) 10

  (G) 20

  (H) 30

  (J) 25

27. **If no students leave Highview School and no new students enroll, how many third graders will there be next year?**

  (A) 45

  (B) 30

  (C) 40

  (D) 35

STOP

Published by Spectrum. Copyright protected.

1-57768-974-7 *Spectrum Test Practice 4*

SCIENCE

● Lesson 1: Concepts

Directions: Read each item. Choose the correct answer for the question and mark the space next to it.

Examples

A. When water freezes, it changes from —

- Ⓐ a gas to a solid.
- Ⓑ a liquid to a gas.
- Ⓒ a liquid to a solid.
- Ⓓ a solid to a gas.

B. Which of these is living?

- Ⓕ rock
- Ⓖ flower
- Ⓗ glass
- Ⓙ water

 Clue If you are not sure which answer is correct, take your best guess. Eliminate answer choices you know are wrong.

● Practice

1. **What is the name of the primary blood circulation organ in the human body?**
   - Ⓐ liver
   - Ⓑ stomach
   - Ⓒ brain
   - Ⓓ heart

2. **When a girl starts running, she is converting stored energy into —**
   - Ⓕ heat energy.
   - Ⓖ sound energy.
   - Ⓗ kinetic energy.
   - Ⓙ light energy.

3. **What is the name of the substance that flows out of a volcano?**
   - Ⓐ magma
   - Ⓑ lava
   - Ⓒ ash
   - Ⓓ crater

4. **Which of the following does a plant cell have that an animal cell doesn't?**
   - Ⓕ mitochondria
   - Ⓖ chloroplasts
   - Ⓗ nucleus
   - Ⓙ cell membrane

5. **Which of the following is a chemical change?**
   - Ⓐ ice cream melting in the sun
   - Ⓑ crushing a soda can
   - Ⓒ mixing salt and sugar
   - Ⓓ burning wood in the fireplace

6. **What will happen between these two magnets?**

N	S	N	S

   - Ⓕ attract
   - Ⓖ repel
   - Ⓗ not move
   - Ⓙ None of these

STOP

SCIENCE

● Lesson 2: Applications

Directions: Read the selection. Answer the questions using complete sentences.

Example

Dinosaurs were vertebrates. A vertebrate is an animal that has a backbone. A backbone is made of many smaller bones, called vertebrae. The vertebrae are connected to each other. Humans and all other mammals, reptiles, birds, fish, and amphibians that live today are vertebrates.

A.   What do modern mammals have in common with dinosaurs?

_____

_____

_____

 Clue   Read carefully. Circle any words you don't understand and come back to them later.

● Practice

Why Are There Seasons?

Earth revolves around the sun. It also spins on an invisible axis that runs through its center.

It takes $365\frac{1}{4}$ days, or one year, for the Earth to revolve once around the sun. Just as the moon moves in an orbit around Earth, Earth moves around the sun. The Earth does not move in a perfect circle. Its orbit is an ellipse, which is a flattened circle, like an oval. As Earth revolves around the sun in an elliptical shape, it spins on its invisible axis.

Earth's axis of rotation is not straight up and down, it is tilted. This important feature produces the seasons on Earth. No matter where Earth is in its rotation around the sun, its axis is tilted in the same direction and at the same angle. So, as Earth moves, different parts of it are facing the sun and different parts are facing away. The North Pole is tilting toward the sun in June, so the northern half of Earth is enjoying summer. In December, the North Pole

is tilted away from the sun, so the northern part of the world experiences winter.

This important relationship between Earth and the sun determines how hot and cold we are, when we plants our crops, and whether we have droughts or floods.

1.   **If North America is having summer, what season would the Australians be enjoying and why?**

_____

_____

_____

2.   **What do you think would happen if Earth's axis were not tilted, but straight up and down?**

_____

_____

_____

STOP

ANSWER SHEET

Published by Spectrum. Copyright protected.

STUDENT'S NAME		SCHOOL

LAST   FIRST   MI

TEACHER

FEMALE ◯   MALE ◯

BIRTH DATE

MONTH	DAY	YEAR

JAN ◯
FEB ◯
MAR ◯
APR ◯
MAY ◯
JUN ◯
JUL ◯
AUG ◯
SEP ◯
OCT ◯
NOV ◯
DEC ◯

GRADE

③ ④ ⑤

SCIENCE

A	Ⓐ Ⓑ Ⓒ Ⓓ
1	Ⓐ Ⓑ Ⓒ Ⓓ
2	Ⓕ Ⓖ Ⓗ Ⓙ
3	Ⓐ Ⓑ Ⓒ Ⓓ
4	Ⓕ Ⓖ Ⓗ Ⓙ
5	Ⓐ Ⓑ Ⓒ Ⓓ
6	Ⓕ Ⓖ Ⓗ Ⓙ
7	Ⓐ Ⓑ Ⓒ Ⓓ
8	Ⓕ Ⓖ Ⓗ Ⓙ

1-57768-974-7 *Spectrum Test Practice 4*

Name _____ Date_____

SCIENCE PRACTICE TEST

● **Directions:** Read each item or passage. Choose the correct answer for the question and mark the space next to it, or write a response.

Example

A. Why do reptiles spend a lot of time in the sun?

(A) They are cold-blooded.
(B) The sun changes their skin color to help them hide.
(C) They live in the desert.
(D) The sun helps them produce food.

1. What two forces cause erosion?
   (A) water and gravity
   (B) sun and wind
   (C) wind and water
   (D) gravity and wind

2. Which label is missing from the drawing?
   (F) coil filament
   (G) circuit
   (H) terminal
   (J) plug

   base
   glass bulb
   wire support   glass support

3. Which of the following would decompose most quickly?
   (A) apple
   (B) shell
   (C) rock
   (D) bone

4. If you wanted to lift a heavy crate up into the air, which would be the best simple machine to use?
   (F) screw
   (G) lever
   (H) pulley
   (J) inclined plane

5. The drawing below shows a _____ circuit.
   (A) parallel
   (B) series
   (C) cross
   (D) open

6. Earthquakes are caused by —
   (F) static electricity.
   (G) El Niño.
   (H) severe weather conditions.
   (J) plates on the earth's surface moving.

7. Which organ is the command center of the body?
   (A) bladder
   (B) heart
   (C) brain
   (D) liver

8. What causes the tide?
   (F) pull of gravity between Earth and the moon
   (G) pull of gravity among Earth, the moon, and Mars
   (H) pull of gravity among Earth, the moon, and the sun
   (J) pull of gravity between Earth and the sun

GO ON

Read the selection. Answer the questions using complete sentences.

Cells of Living Things

Cells are the smallest and most basic units of living matter. They are the small pieces that when put together make organs, plants, and even people. All living things are made of cells, though not all cells are exactly alike.

Both animal and plant cells have a cell membrane, which holds all the cell parts together. The nucleus is one of the largest parts of the cell. It is the command center of the cell and controls the activities in the cell. Chromosomes inside this command center control what an organism will be like. For instance, your chromosomes carry the information that makes you have blue or brown eyes or black or red hair. Cytoplasm is the gooey stuff that all the parts of the cell float in. It's mostly water, but also has some important chemicals inside. Both plant and animal cells have mitochondria, which is where food is burned to give the cell energy.

Animal and plants cells also have some differences. The plant cell has a cell wall, just outside the cell membrane, that makes the cell stiff. Both animal and plant cells have vacuoles, but animals have far more and they are much smaller. Finally, plant cells have chloroplasts. This is where the cell produces chlorophyll. This chemical makes food for the plant when the sunlight hits it. This is how a plant feeds itself.

While animals and plants cells have similarities and differences, one thing is certain. Without cells, the basic building blocks, living things would not exist.

9. **What is the role of the nucleus in a cell?**

_____

_____

_____

_____

_____

10. **What is the role of chromosomes in the cell?**

_____

_____

_____

_____

11. **Why do you think plants cells contain chloroplasts and animal cells do not?**

_____

_____

_____

_____

SOCIAL STUDIES

● **Lesson 1: Concepts**

Directions: Read each item. Choose the correct answer to the question and mark the space next to it.

Examples

A. Where should you look to find the meaning of symbols on a map?	**B.** Which of the following does not help describe the Midwest states?
(A) key	(F) forests
(B) compass rose	(G) fertile
(C) scale	(H) mountains
(D) latitude lines	(J) many lakes

 Clue If you are not sure which answer is correct, take your best guess. Eliminate answer choices you know are wrong.

● **Practice**

1. **Which state does this outline show?**

   (A) Michigan
   (B) Florida
   (C) New York
   (D) California

2. **Which of the following is the postal abbreviation for Indiana?**

   (F) ID
   (G) IA
   (H) IN
   (J) IL

3. **What is a deep valley with steep sides?**

   (A) hill
   (B) mountain
   (C) canyon
   (D) basin

4. **What is the climate zone of Michigan?**

   (F) desert
   (G) mediterranean
   (H) tropical
   (J) continental

5. **The park is _____ of the store.**

   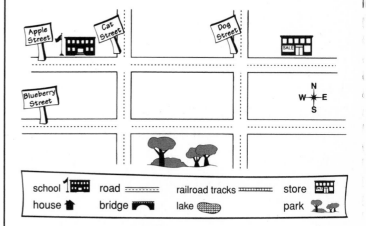

   school 🏫 road ======= railroad tracks ▬▬▬▬▬ store 🏬
   house 🏠 bridge ⌒ lake 🌊 park 🌳

   (A) southwest
   (B) northeast
   (C) southeast
   (D) eastsouth

Name _____ Date_____

SOCIAL STUDIES

● **Lesson 2: Applications**

Directions: Read the selection. Answer the questions using complete sentences.

Example

There are many different landforms on Earth. Mountains and hills are where the land has been pushed up. They have peaks and valleys. A plateau is a piece of land that rises above sea level but has a flat top, unlike a mountain. A plain is a low area of land that is fairly flat.

A.   **Explain the similarities and differences between plateaus and plains.**

_____

_____

_____

 Clue   **Read carefully. Circle any words you don't understand and come back to them later.**

● **Practice**

Native American Life in the Northeast

Before Europeans arrived in the Northeast, thick forests covered the land. The Native Americans, including the Iroquois, the Wampanoag, and the Mahicans, made these forests their home.

During the winter, the Native Americans stayed close to home, telling stories, playing games, and living off the food they had collected earlier in the year. As the weather warmed, they fished in rivers and streams, gathered eggs, and hunted geese and other birds.

In the spring, the Native Americans also planted corn, beans, and pumpkins. They gathered wild fruit, herbs, and tree bark to use as medicines.

August was a time of harvest. The Native Americans would leave their villages and set out to hunt in the woods. The men hunted for

bear, deer, and other game. The meat was dried and saved for the cold winter months.

The villagers returned home at the first sign of snow. The Native Americans relied on the forest to live and gave thanks for the food and shelter they had gotten from it.

1.   **What were the ways in which the Native Americans prepared for winter?**

_____

_____

2.   **How do you think the life of Europeans differed from that of the Native Americans at this time?**

_____

_____

STOP

STUDENT'S NAME		
LAST	FIRST	MI

SCHOOL

TEACHER

FEMALE ○   MALE ○

BIRTH DATE

MONTH	DAY	YEAR

JAN ○
FEB ○
MAR ○
APR ○
MAY ○
JUN ○
JUL ○
AUG ○
SEP ○
OCT ○
NOV ○
DEC ○

GRADE
③ ④ ⑤

SOCIAL STUDIES

A Ⓐ Ⓑ Ⓒ Ⓓ   **3** Ⓐ Ⓑ Ⓒ Ⓓ   **6** Ⓕ Ⓖ Ⓗ Ⓙ

1 Ⓐ Ⓑ Ⓒ Ⓓ   **4** Ⓕ Ⓖ Ⓗ Ⓙ   **7** Ⓐ Ⓑ Ⓒ Ⓓ

2 Ⓕ Ⓖ Ⓗ Ⓙ   **5** Ⓐ Ⓑ Ⓒ Ⓓ

Name _____   Date _____

SOCIAL STUDIES PRACTICE TEST

● **Directions:** Read each item or passage. Choose the correct answer to the question and mark the space next to it, or write a response.

Example

A. **Which of the following features best fits in the mountain states?**

    Ⓐ coasts

    Ⓑ plains

    Ⓒ beaches

    Ⓓ canyons

---

1. **Which compass rose below is labeled correctly?**

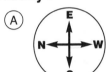 

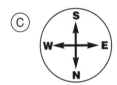 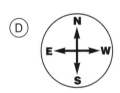

2. **The population of a state tells —**

    Ⓕ what ethnic groups live there.

    Ⓖ what the weather is like there.

    Ⓗ how much money is made there.

    Ⓙ how many people live there.

3. **Which of these is not a coastal state?**

    Ⓐ Oregon

    Ⓑ Maine

    Ⓒ Florida

    Ⓓ Missouri

4. **What is a body of land surrounded by water on three sides?**

    Ⓕ plain

    Ⓖ peninsula

    Ⓗ plateau

    Ⓙ island

5. **If the United States is having winter, New Zealand is having —**

    Ⓐ winter

    Ⓑ spring

    Ⓒ summer

    Ⓓ fall

6. **Which of the following is not a natural resource?**

    Ⓕ water

    Ⓖ coal

    Ⓗ wind

    Ⓙ automobiles

7.

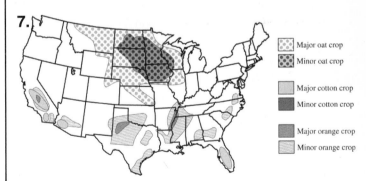

Major oat crop
Minor oat crop
Major cotton crop
Minor cotton crop
Major orange crop
Minor orange crop

Which of these states grows a minor crop of oats?

    Ⓐ Florida

    Ⓑ Texas

    Ⓒ South Dakota

    Ⓓ Idaho

GO ON ➤

═══════ SOCIAL STUDIES PRACTICE TEST (CONT.) ═══════

Read the selection. Answer the questions using complete sentences.

Producing Grapes in California

California is a state teeming with life. Not only is it one of the most populous states, it is also one of the country's major farming states. Despite the lack of water in California, farmers have managed to make it a very fertile area.

Fruits and vegetables grow well in California, and among these is grapes. You may have heard of the California raisins, but they also *produce* fresh grapes, juice, and wine. California supplies the majority of the grapes in the United States.

In the winter, cuttings from mature grape plants are buried to make new plants. The grapevines are nurtured until they are old enough to produce grapes. Grapes are harvested in the summer and fall. The bunches are carefully cut by hand. This work requires a lot of *labor*. Many *migrant workers* are brought into the state from other areas and from Central America. The money that migrant workers *earn* is very useful to their families, who may live in far less abundant regions.

Wine and grapes are sent to a winery to be crushed. The juice is aged and then bottled for sale. Raisin grapes are dried in the sun in the vineyard. Once they are ready, they are packaged by workers in a *factory* and sent to *stores* for sale to *consumers*. Fresh grapes are carefully packed, treated to prevent decay, and placed in refrigerated trucks or railroad cars. These vehicles will *transport* their *goods* to their final destination—your neighborhood supermarket.

Grape and other vegetable farming provides needed *income* for both resident and migrant workers in the state of California.

8. **How do grape farms and other farms help the people of California?**

_____

_____

_____

_____

_____

9. **What is the meaning of the word *consumers* as it is used in this selection?**

_____

_____

_____

_____

10. **What might happen to the migrant workers if California stopped producing grapes?**

_____

_____

_____

_____

STOP

READING: VOCABULARY
Lesson 1: Synonyms
• Page 11
- A. C
- B. G
- 1. C
- 2. F
- 3. C
- 4. G
- 5. D
- 6. F
- 7. A
- 8. H

READING: VOCABULARY
Lesson 2: Vocabulary Skills
• Page 12
- A. A
- B. J
- 1. B
- 2. H
- 3. A
- 4. H
- 5. A
- 6. F
- 7. B

READING: VOCABULARY
Lesson 3: Antonyms
• Page 13
- A. B
- B. F
- 1. B
- 2. G
- 3. C
- 4. F
- 5. C
- 6. F
- 7. A
- 8. F

READING: VOCABULARY
Lesson 4: Multi-Meaning Words
• Page 14
- A. D
- 1. D
- 2. H
- 3. A
- 4. H
- 5. D

READING: VOCABULARY
Lesson 5: Words in Context
• Page 15
- A. D
- B. F
- 1. B
- 2. H
- 3. D
- 4. H
- 5. D
- 6. G

READING: VOCABULARY
Lesson 6: Word Study
• Page 16
- A. B
- B. G
- 1. B
- 2. F
- 3. A
- 4. G

- 5. B
- 6. J

READING: VOCABULARY
SAMPLE TEST
• Pages 17–20
- A. B
- B. H
- 1. A
- 2. J
- 3. B
- 4. H
- 5. C
- 6. H
- 7. A
- 8. J
- 9. A
- 10. F
- 11. C
- 12. F
- 13. C
- 14. H
- 15. A
- 16. J
- 17. A
- 18. G
- 19. B
- 20. G
- 21. D
- 22. J
- 23. B
- 24. H
- 25. D
- 26. J
- 27. B
- 28. H
- 29. A
- 30. J
- 31. B
- 32. F
- 33. C
- 34. J

READING: READING COMPREHENSION
Lesson 7: Main Idea
• Page 21
- A. B
- 1. D
- 2. F

READING: READING COMPREHENSION
Lesson 8: Recalling Details/Sequencing
• Page 22
- A. D
- 1. D
- 2. H
- 3. A

READING: READING COMPREHENSION
Lesson 9: Inferencing/Drawing Conclusions
• Page 23
- A. C
- 1. B
- 2. G

READING: READING COMPREHENSION
Lesson 10: Fact & Opinion/Cause & Effect
• Page 24
- A. D
- 1. D
- 2. F

READING: READING COMPREHENSION
Lesson 11: Parts of a Story
• Page 25
- A. B
- 1. A
- 2. F
- 3. D

READING: READING COMPREHENSION
Lesson 12: Fiction
• Page 26
- A. C
- 1. A
- 2. H
- 3. D

READING: READING COMPREHENSION
Lesson 13: Fiction
• Page 27
- A. C
- 1. A
- 2. G
- 3. C

READING: READING COMPREHENSION
Lesson 14: Fiction
• Pages 28–29
- A. A
- 1. B
- 2. H
- 3. C
- 4. J
- 5. A
- 6. H

READING: READING COMPREHENSION
Lesson 15: Fiction
• Pages 30–31
- A. B
- 1. A
- 2. H
- 3. D
- 4. H
- 5. A
- 6. G

READING: READING COMPREHENSION
Lesson 16: Nonfiction
• Page 32
- A. A
- 1. C
- 2. F
- 3. A

READING: READING COMPREHENSION
Lesson 17: Nonfiction
• Page 33
- A. C

1. D
2. G
3. D

READING: READING COMPREHENSION

Lesson 18: Nonfiction
• Pages 34–35

A. D
1. B
2. F
3. C
4. F
5. C
6. G

READING: READING COMPREHENSION

Lesson 19: Nonfiction
• Pages 36–37

A. B
1. C
2. J
3. B
4. J
5. D
6. F

READING: READING COMPREHENSION SAMPLE TEST

• Pages 38–43

A. A
1. C
2. J
3. A
4. J
5. C
6. F
7. B
8. H
9. A
10. F
11. C
12. G
13. A
14. F
15. D
16. J
17. D

READING: READING PRACTICE TEST

Part 1: Vocabulary
• Pages 45–48

A. B
B. H
1. A
2. J
3. C
4. F
5. B
6. F
7. D
8. G
9. A
10. G
11. C
12. F
13. B
14. H
15. A

16. J
17. D
18. J
19. B
20. J
21. C
22. J
23. C
24. F
25. A
26. H
27. B
28. F
29. C
30. G
31. A
32. J
33. C

Part 2: Fiction
• Pages 49–52

A. A
1. C
2. H
3. B
4. J
5. B
6. H
7. A
8. H
9. D
10. G
11. B
12. H

Part 3: Nonfiction
• Pages 53–57

A. D
1. C
2. J
3. B
4. J
5. A
6. F
7. C
8. J
9. D
10. G
11. D
12. H
13. C
14. G
15. A

LANGUAGE: LANGUAGE MECHANICS

Lesson 1: Punctuation
• Pages 58–59

A. C
B. H
1. D
2. H
3. D
4. H
5. B
6. H
7. A
8. J
9. C
10. H

11. C
12. G
13. A
14. H
15. D

LANGUAGE: LANGUAGE MECHANICS

Lesson 2: Capitalization & Punctuation
• Pages 60–62

A. C
B. H
1. A
2. F
3. B
4. G
5. D
6. J
7. A
8. H
9. B
10. F
11. C
12. J
13. B
14. F
15. B
16. J
17. C
18. F
19. B

LANGUAGE: LANGUAGE MECHANICS SAMPLE TEST

• Pages 63-66

A. C
1. D
2. G
3. C
4. J
5. B
6. G
7. A
8. J
9. C
10. G
11. D
12. G
13. B
14. F
15. B
16. J
17. C
18. H
19. D
20. G
21. B
22. H
23. D
24. H
25. A
26. H
27. B
28. J

ANSWER KEY

LANGUAGE: LANGUAGE EXPRESSION
Lesson 3: Usage
• Pages 67-69
A. D
B. G
1. B
2. J
3. D
4. J
5. C
6. G
7. B
8. J
9. B
10. G
11. A
12. F
13. B
14. H
15. A
16. G
17. D
18. F
19. C
20. G

LANGUAGE: LANGUAGE EXPRESSION
Lesson 4: Sentences
• Pages 70–72
A. A
B. H
1. A
2. G
3. A
4. G
5. A
6. G
7. C
8. H
9. B
10. J
11. C
12. G
13. B
14. J

LANGUAGE: LANGUAGE EXPRESSION
Lesson 5: Paragraphs
• Pages 73–76
A. C
1. B
2. G
3. D
4. J
5. D
6. F
7. B
8. G
9. B
10. G
11. A
12. G
13. C

LANGUAGE: LANGUAGE EXPRESSION SAMPLE TEST
• Pages 77–80
A. C
1. C
2. F
3. C
4. G
5. B
6. G
7. B
8. H
9. D
10. G
11. C
12. F
13. C
14. J
15. B
16. H
17. D
18. F
19. D
20. H

LANGUAGE: SPELLING
Lesson 6: Spelling Skills
• Pages 81–82
A. A
B. H
1. D
2. G
3. D
4. G
5. B
6. G
7. A
8. F
9. C
10. H
11. A
12. G
13. D
14. G
15. D
16. F
17. B

LANGUAGE: SPELLING SKILLS SAMPLE TEST
• Pages 83–84
A. B
B. F
1. D
2. J
3. A
4. G
5. D
6. F
7. C
8. G
9. A
10. G
11. C
12. F
13. A
14. H
15. D
16. F

17. C
18. J
19. A

LANGUAGE: STUDY SKILLS
Lesson 7: Study Skills
• Pages 85–86
A. D
1. B
2. F
3. C
4. F
5. D
6. F
7. D
8. H

LANGUAGE: STUDY SKILLS SAMPLE TEST
• Pages 87–89
A. D
B. F
1. B
2. F
3. D
4. G
5. C
6. F
7. B
8. J
9. C
10. G
11. C
12. J
13. C
14. H
15. A

LANGUAGE: LANGUAGE PRACTICE TEST
Part 1: Language Mechanics
• Pages 91–93
A. A
1. C
2. G
3. A
4. J
5. B
6. G
7. B
8. G
9. D
10. H
11. A
12. G
13. C
14. J
15. B
16. F
17. B
18. F
19. C
20. H

Part 2: Language Expression
• Pages 94–97
A. A
1. A
2. H
3. A
4. F

5. D
6. G
7. B
8. H
9. D
10. G
11. B
12. H
13. C
14. F
15. B
16. J
17. A
18. G
19. B
20. J

Part 3: Spelling
• Pages 98–99

A. B
B. J
1. D
2. H
3. C
4. J
5. B
6. H
7. A
8. J
9. B
10. G
11. C
12. F
13. A
14. G
15. C
16. G
17. B
18. H
19. D

Part 4: Study Skills
• Pages 100–101

A. C
1. B
2. H
3. C
4. J
5. C
6. G
7. D
8. G
9. B
10. G
11. D
12. H
13. A
14. G

MATH: CONCEPTS
Lesson 1: Numeration
• Pages 102–103

A. B
B. G
1. C
2. J
3. C
4. F
5. C
6. J

7. B
8. F
9. C
10. H
11. B
12. H
13. D

MATH: CONCEPTS
Lesson 2: Number Concepts
• Pages 104–105

A. B
B. F
1. D
2. H
3. C
4. G
5. C
6. H
7. D
8. J
9. A
10. H
11. D
12. G
13. C
14. G

MATH: CONCEPTS
Lesson 3: Properties
• Pages 106–107

A. B
B. H
1. C
2. H
3. D
4. G
5. C
6. J
7. D
8. F
9. B
10. F
11. B
12. H

MATH: CONCEPTS
Lesson 4: Fractions & Decimals
• Pages 108–109

A. C
B. F
1. D
2. F
3. A
4. H
5. D
6. J
7. B
8. F
9. A
10. G
11. A
12. F

MATH: CONCEPTS SAMPLE TEST
• Pages 110–111

A. C
B. F
1. A
2. J

3. D
4. G
5. D
6. F
7. C
8. J
9. D
10. F
11. D
12. G

MATH: COMPUTATION
Lesson 5: Addition & Subtraction of Whole Numbers
• Page 112

A. B
B. F
1. D
2. H
3. C
4. F
5. A
6. G
7. A
8. H

MATH: COMPUTATION
Lesson 6: Addition & Subtraction of Fractions
• Pages 113–114

A. B
B. G
1. B
2. H
3. B
4. H
5. A
6. H
7. C
8. F
9. A
10. G
11. A
12. H
13. B
14. F
15. B
16. G

MATH: COMPUTATION
Lesson 7: Addition & Subtraction of Decimals
• Page 115

A. A
B. G
1. A
2. G
3. B
4. F
5. B
6. H
7. C
8. H

MATH: COMPUTATION
Lesson 8: Multiplication of Whole Numbers
• Page 116

A. B
B. F
1. A

2. H
3. C
4. G
5. C
6. H
7. D
8. G

MATH: COMPUTATION
Lesson 9: Division of Whole Numbers
• Page 117

A. C
B. J
1. A
2. F
3. A
4. G
5. B
6. G
7. B
8. G

MATH: COMPUTATION SAMPLE TEST
• Pages 118–119

A. A
B. J
1. A
2. H
3. B
4. H
5. C
6. H
7. B
8. F
9. A
10. F
11. B
12. J
13. A
14. J
15. C
16. H
17. A
18. G
19. B
20. H
21. A
22. H

MATH: APPLICATIONS
Lesson 10: Geometry
• Pages 120–122

A. B
1. C
2. G
3. D
4. J
5. C
6. F
7. C
8. H
9. A
10. G
11. D
12. F
13. C
14. J

MATH: APPLICATIONS
Lesson 11: Measurement
• Pages 123–126

A. C
B. H
1. C
2. F
3. D
4. J
5. B
6. J
7. D
8. J
9. D
10. G
11. B
12. G
13. D
14. F
15. D
16. H
17. C
18. H
19. D
20. J
21. A
22. G
23. C
24. G
25. D
26. H
27. D

MATH: APPLICATIONS
Lesson 12: Problem Solving
• Pages 127–130

A. C
1. D
2. G
3. A
4. G
5. A
6. J
7. D
8. J
9. D
10. H
11. D
12. G
13. A
14. F
15. D
16. J
17. B
18. H
19. A
20. J

MATH: APPLICATIONS SAMPLE TEST
• Pages 131–134

A. D
B. J
1. C
2. H
3. B
4. F
5. C
6. J

7. D
8. G
9. B
10. J
11. A
12. H
13. B
14. F
15. A
16. H
17. B
18. G
19. A
20. G
21. C
22. F
23. A
24. J
25. B
26. F

MATH: MATH PRACTICE TEST
Part 1: Concepts
• Pages 136–138

A. A
B. G
1. D
2. F
3. C
4. J
5. C
6. H
7. B
8. F
9. C
10. F
11. B
12. F
13. C
14. H
15. C
16. H
17. B
18. G
19. C
20. H
21. D

Part 2: Computation
• Pages 139–140

A. B
B. F
1. A
2. G
3. A
4. H
5. D
6. H
7. B
8. H
9. C
10. F
11. B
12. H
13. C
14. G
15. A
16. F
17. B

18. H
19. D
20. F
21. D
22. G

Part 3: Applications
• Pages 141–144
A. A
1. C
2. J
3. C
4. J
5. C
6. G
7. A
8. H
9. A
10. F
11. C
12. J
13. C
14. J
15. C
16. G
17. D
18. F
19. B
20. F
21. C
22. J
23. D
24. G
25. B
26. J
27. D

SCIENCE
Lesson 1: Concepts
• Page 145
A. C
B. G
1. D
2. H
3. B
4. G
5. D
6. F

SCIENCE
Lesson 2: Applications
• Page 146
A. Dinosaurs and mammals are alike because they both have backbones that help support their bodies.
1. Winter, because at that time of year the southern half of Earth is tilted away from the sun and therefore receives less direct light from the sun.
2. If Earth's axis were straight up and down, the seasons and amount of sunlight would be the same, both in the northern and southern halves of Earth.

SCIENCE PRACTICE TEST
• Pages 148–149
A. A
1. C

2. F
3. A
4. H
5. B
6. J
7. C
8. F
9. The nucleus of a cell controls all the activities within a cell.
10. Chromosomes determine the characteristics of an organism. In the human, this would be eye and hair color and other traits.
11. Animals do not contain chloroplasts because they get their food from vegetables, meats, and grains, and they don't need sunlight to make energy.

SOCIAL STUDIES
Lesson 1: Concepts
• Page 150
A. A
B. H
1. D
2. H
3. C
4. J
5. A

SOCIAL STUDIES
Lesson 2: Applications
• Page 151
A. Plateaus and plains are both rather flat on the top. However, plateaus are usually much higher above sea level than plains.
1. They gathered fish, herbs, and eggs. They hunted birds, bear, and deer and dried the meat. They planted crops. They stored all this food to help them get through the winter.
2. Europeans may not have had to make as many preparations for winter as the Native Americans because of food and other goods they could find in markets. Also, they may not have relied on the forest as much as the Native Americans. They would have been able to get goods from many places in the world.

SOCIAL STUDIES: SOCIAL STUDIES PRACTICE TEST
• Pages 153–154
A. D
1. B
2. J
3. D
4. G
5. C
6. J
7. C
8. These farms supply jobs, which in turn provide income. They also provide valuable goods for the California and U.S. marketplace.

9. *Consumers* refers to the people who buy the goods (in this case, grape products) in the supermarket or other store.
10. Though grapes are not California's only crop, stopping the production of grapes would reduce the number of jobs available for migrant workers. This would affect the native community in which the worker lives as well as the worker's family because the flow of money could slow or cease. This worker would then be less able to purchase goods and services in his native community.